Mrs Beeton's

Jam-making and Preserves

Including:

Preserves, Marmalades, Pickles and Home-Made Wines

400 Recipes

Copyright © RHE Media Ltd 2016
This book was first published in 1924. This edition published in 2016 by:
RHE Media Ltd
5 Pennsylvania Crescent
Exeter
EX4 4SF
www.wordstothewise.co.uk

ISBN 978-1-910226-18-6 (eBook-Kindle)
ISBN 978-1-910226-19-3 (eBook-ePub)
ISBN 978-1-910226-49-0 (Paperback)

All rights reserved. No part of this book may be reprinted or reproduced or utilized in any form or by any electronic, mechanical, or other means, now known or hereafter invented, including photocopying and recording, or in any information storage or retrieval system, without permission in writing from RHE Media Ltd.
Disclaimer: This is a Vintage Words of Wisdom title. As such, any recipes and/or medical, scientific, technological or legal advice and guidance contained herein are likely to be out-of-date. Therefore, before carrying out any of the procedures recommended in this book please check the most recent guidance available and/or consult an expert on the latest methods, treatments, guidelines, legislation, etc. RHE Media Ltd bears no responsibility or liability whatsoever for any loss, injury or damage caused by using and/or following any recipes and/or medical, scientific, technological or legal advice and guidance given in this book.

Acknowledgements:
Page 36 - Photo by Dennis Jarvis from Halifax, Canada. Creative Commons Attribution-Share Alike 2.0 Generic licence
Cover painting: Nature morte aux poires by Olivier Duchâteau

British Library Cataloguing in Publication Data
A catalogue record for this book is available from the British Library

Print and bind by Short Run Press Limited, Bittern Road, Sowton Industrial Estate, Exeter, Devon, EX2 7LW, UK.

www.wordstothewise.co.uk

CONTENTS

PUBLISHER'S FOREWORD   *iv*
RECIPE INDEX   *viii*

I	THE ART OF PRESERVING	1
II	RECIPES FOR JAMS AND PRESERVES	11
III	RECIPES FOR MARMALADES	23
IV	RECIPES FOR FRUIT JELLIES	29
V	PRESERVED AND CRYSTALLIZED FRUITS	37
VI	BOTTLING FRUIT	51
VII	FRUITS IN BRANDY	57
VIII	FRUIT PASTES AND CURDS	59
IX	SYRUPS AND FRUIT JUICES	63
X	PICKLES	67
XI	MISCELLANEOUS PRESERVES AND PICKLES	85
XII	STORE OR CONDIMENT SAUCES	89
XIII	HOME-MADE WINES AND FRUIT SYRUPS	101
XIV	LIQUEURS	113

INTRODUCTION TO THE VINTAGE WORDS OF WISDOM SERIES   *122*

PUBLISHER'S FOREWORD

THIS USEFUL RECIPE BOOK from the 1920s includes 400 recipes for jams, jellies, pickles, chutneys, and wines. It also provides detailed guidance on all aspects of preserving, bottling, sterilising, drying and crystallising fruits. The recipes are based on those by Mrs Beeton (including the now famous carrot jam) and they have been updated to include advances in techniques that were common in the early twentieth century. Familiar recipes are included alongside more exotic preserves like Harvey Sauce, Cucumber Ketchup, Hawthorn Liqueur and Maidenhair Syrup, making this an entertaining and exciting preserving adventure!

Mrs Beeton's Jam-making and Preserves provides a fascinating insight into skills and methods that were in use before the invention of the food processor and electric hob, and before the presence of a refrigerator in every home. Among other methods, jars of jam are sealed with paper brushed with the white of an egg and some vegetable preserves are topped with clarified mutton fat to create an air-tight seal, the preparation of some ingredients takes many days, and the quantities of sugar, for example, many surprise the modern jam-maker. However, all these recipes can be adapted to suit modern tastes and to take advantage of modern technology. Though perhaps not for the beginner, this book offers a wealth of preserving challenges for the confident cook. From recipes for ingredients not commonly used today to unusual combinations and preserves that, quite frankly, sound disgusting and/or positively dangerous (have a look at the Mustapha Ketchup recipe – try at your own risk!), this collation is an enjoyable exploration of the history of preserving and a rare opportunity to experience the tastes that a previous generation enjoyed.

ADVICE AND SAFETY FIRST

Weights and measures conversions

There are plenty of useful conversion charts available online (see, for example, **http://www.deliciousmagazine.co.uk/articles/cooking-conversion-tables** or, for a more historical guide, see **http://gwydir.demon.co.uk/jo/units/volume.htm**) and in other recipe books so we won't go into a great deal of detail, but here is a brief guide. Ingredients in this book are measured in old British Imperial units:

Ounces (oz) – 1 oz. is 25 gms.
Pounds (lb.) – 1 lb. is 450 gms.
Saltspoons – a saltspoon is a ¼ of a teaspoon or 1.2 ml.
Mustardspoons – the only reference I can find to this quantity suggests that it is about 200 mg. However, the internet informs me that it is a surprisingly common measurement, used for everything from (obviously) mustard to medicines. Therefore, I can only assume that more people have mustard spoons than I would imagine!
Teaspoons – 1 teaspoon is 5 ml. In one recipe it refers to an eighth of a teaspoonful, which is a definitely just a pinch!
Dessertspoons – 1 dessertspoonful is 10 ml. or 2 teaspoons.
Tablespoons – 1 tablespoon is 15 ml (or 3 teaspoons).
Gill – 1 gill is 5 fluid ounces or 1.42 ml. There are 4 gills to the pint. The Imperial gill is 1.2 US gills.
Pints – 1 pint is an eighth of a gallon, 20 Imperial fluid ounces or 568 ml. (please note that a US pint is 16 fluid ounces or 473 ml.). The other way round, I remember the conversion of litres to pints as 'a litre of water is a pint and three-quarters' – it sticks in my brain this way.
Quarts – 1 quart is 2 pints (a 'quart'er of a gallon) or 1.14 litres.
Gallons – 1 gallon is 8 pints or 4.55 litres. The US gallon is 3.79 litres.

Glossary

Baysalt – this is sea salt (e.g. Maldon sea salt) – i.e. salt from the bay.
Capillaire – a syrup or infusion of the Maidenhair fern (for more details visit **http://www.theoldfoodie.com/2008/05/on-capillaire.html**).
Capsicum – these are sweet peppers.
Clary – the flowers of the clary sage plant (for more details visit, for example, **http://theherbgardener.blogspot.co.uk/2011/05/how-to-grow-clary-sage.html**)
Cowslips – remember that, while not illegal, it is not advisable to pick great quantities of wild flowers. Cowslips are not as common as they were when this book was written (though I don't think that cowslip wine makers are to blame!) so they should be allowed to flower in peace so that they can disperse their seeds far and wide. It is illegal in the UK to uproot wild flower plants in order to transfer them to your own garden.

Radish Pods

Gum arabic – also known as acacia gum, this is used today by the food industry as a stabiliser (E414). It is used as an edible glue and binder, an emulsifier and thickening agent. It is available to buy online.

Isinglass – made from the dried swim bladders of fish, this is a form of collagen used for the clarification of wine and beer. Drinks made using isinglass are therefore not acceptable to many vegetarians and all vegans, but there are vegan alternatives such as Bentonite and Irish moss.

Racking – siphoning off wine from the lees (sediment) into another vessel. There are plenty of websites on wine-making that provide more details.

Radish pods – if radish plants are allowed to bolt they produce seed pods. These seed pods are edible – they taste like radishes, crunchy and delicious. In Indian cuisine they are known as mogri or moongre.

Equipment

Sugar (candy) thermometer – this is a vital piece of equipment for many of the recipes in this book. It should be clean and dry before it is put into a pot of hot syrup or it might make the syrup spit. Hot sugar is flammable and sugar burns are nasty.

Preserving pan – this book recommends a copper or brass preserving pan. These are fine if used carefully but the book quite rightly gives a clear warning about not using vinegar in a copper or brass pan and you will notice that it recommends using earthenware vessels to macerate fruit and vegetables. Copper pans react with fruit acid and vinegar to produce toxins. Also, copper pans must be cleaned and dried very carefully or they will develop verdigris – a green pigment composed of various toxic copper compounds. For more information visit, for example, **http://hitchhikingtoheaven.com/2010/06/is-it-safe-to-make-jam-in-a-copper-pan.html** The safest option these days is to use a stainless steel preserving pan. Aluminium is also OK as current research shows that earlier warnings about aluminium and Alzheimer's disease were probably exaggerated. However, there are plenty of good quality stainless steel preserving pans available at reasonable prices, and they are much easier to clean than the older copper or brass pans, though they perhaps have less vintage glamour.

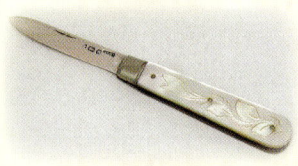

A silver knife – this book was written before stainless steel was in common use. Old steel knives would become stained after exposure to fruit acids and the knife could also taint the fruit. Silver doesn't react to fruit acids so fruit knives were made of silver or silver-plated. However, remember that stain-less doesn't mean stain-proof so, while stainless steel knives are fine for most fruit and vegetables, if they come into contact with very acidic fruit like lemons then they should be cleaned immediately to avoid staining.

Bottles and jam-jars – these days you can buy a wide-variety of glass jars for bottling and for jams, jellies and chutneys. My mother reuses all sorts of glass jars for her jam-making and preserving. As long as they are washed, sterilised and dried properly, and as long as the lids provide an effective air-tight seal, they can be used again and again.

Useful links

One key skill that is required in order to make many of the recipes in this book successfully is the boiling of sugar and the creation of syrups. Here are some useful web links that provide illustrated advice and detailed information on the different degrees of syrup strength.

http://candy.about.com/od/candybasics/a/candytemp.htm
http://baking911.com/quick-guide/how-to-az/candy-sugar-syrup-temperature-chart
http://www.joyofbaking.com/StagesOfCookedSugar.html
http://www.food-info.net/uk/colour/caramel.htm
http://thebakingpan.com/sugar-and-caramel-stages/

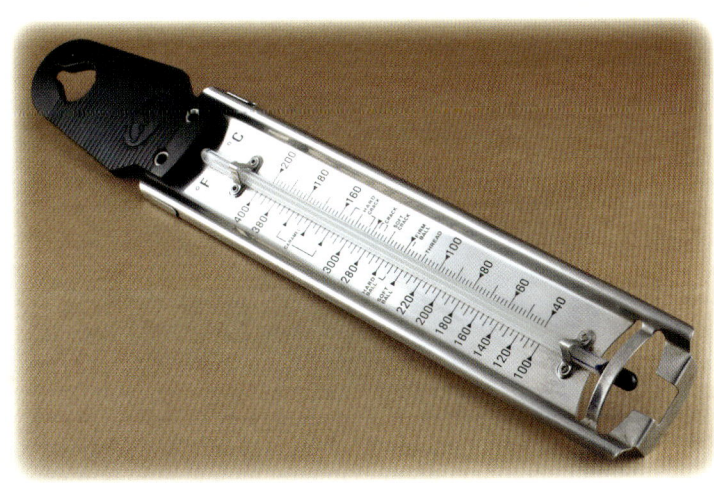

RECIPE INDEX

Almonds

Cox Apples

Almond Syrup	63	Blackberry Jam	13
Anchovies, Essence of	89	Blackberry and Apple Jam	11
Anchovy Ketchup	89	Blackberry Jelly	31
Anise Liqueur	113	Blackberry Syrup	101
Apple and Blackberry Jam	11	Black Currant Jam I & II	13/14
Apple Chutney	68	Black Currant Jelly	31
Apple Ginger I & II	11	Black Currant Liqueur	113
Apple Jam I & II	12	Black Currant Paste	59
Apple Jelly I, II & III	30	Black Currant Wine	104
Apple Marmalade	23	Black Currants in Brandy	57
Apple Paste	59	Blueberries, Pickled	68
Apple and Quince Jam	12	Boar's Head Sauce	89
Apple Wine	101	Boiling the Preserve	4
Apples, to Preserve in Quarters	38	Bottling Fruit & Vegetables	51
Apricot Jam	12	Brine for Pickling	67
Apricot Jam or Marmalade	13	Cabbage, Pickled Red	69
Apricot Jelly	31	Cambridge Sauce	90
Apricot Paste	59	Camp Vinegar	90
Apricot Pulp, Preserved	59	Candied or Glacé Fruits	9
Apricot Wine	101	Capsicums, Pickled I & II	69
Apricots, Bottled	53	Carraway Liqueur	113
Apricots in Brandy	57	Carrick Sauce	90
Apricots, Crystallized	39	Carrot and Beetroot Jam	14
Apricots, Preserved	39	Carrot Jam	14
Arrack Liqueur	113	Carrot Jam (Imitation Apricot)	15
Artichokes, Pickled	68	Cauliflowers, Pickled I & II	70
Banana Jam	13	Cauliflowers, Pickled with Onions	70
Barberries, in Bunches	39	Cayenne Vinegar	90
Barberry Jam	13	Celery Vinegar	90
Barberry Jelly	31	Cherokee	91
Beetroot and Carrot Jam	14	Cherries in Brandy	57
Beetroot Pickle I & II	68	Cherries, Dried	39
Beetroot Preserved	39	Cherries, Pickled I & II	71
Benton Sauce	89	Cherries, to Preserve	40
Bilberries, Pickled	68	Cherries, Red, Bottled	53

Apricots

viii

Mrs Beeton's Jam-making and Preserves

Cherries, Red, Preserved/Crystallized	40	Currant and Gooseberry Jam	16
Cherries, Unsweetened, Bottled	53	Currant and Raspberry Wine	103
Cherries White, Preserved/Crystallized	40	Currant Syrup	63
Cherry Bounce	102	Currant Wine, Black	104
Cherry Brandy	114	Currant Wine, Red	104
Cherry Jam	15	(See also Black Currant, Red and White Currant)	
Cherry Jelly	32		
Cherry Liqueur	114	Currants, Bottled	53
Cherry Wine I & II	102	Currants Spiced	41
Chestnuts, Crystallized	40	Damson Cheese I & II	60
Chilli Vinegar	91	Damson Gin	115
Chutney	71	Damson Jam I & II	15
Chutney, Apple	68	Damson Jelly	32
Chutney, English	71	Damson Paste	60
Chutney, Indian	71	Damson Wine	104
Chutney, Mango	72	Damsons, Baked for Keeping	41
Chutney Sauce, Indian	72	Damsons, Bottled	53/4
Chutney, Tomato	72	Damsons, Pickled	73
Cider	102	Dandelion Wine	105
Citron Liqueur	114	Drying Fruit and Vegetables	49
Citron Marmalade	24	Eggs, Pickled	85
Clary Wine	103	Elderberry Wine	105
Clove Liqueur	114	English Chutney	71
Cockles, Pickled	85	Escaveeke Sauce	91
Covering Pots	6	Excellent Pickle	73
Cowslip Wine	103	Fig Jam	17
Crab-apple Jelly	32	Figs, Preserved	41
Cranberry Jelly	32	Figs, to Preserve	41
Cress Vinegar	91	Fish Condiment Sauce	92
Crystallized Fruits	38	Four Fruit Liqueur	115
Cucumber Ketchup	91	French Beans, Pickled	74
Cucumber Vinegar	91	Fresh Fruit, to Bottle	54
Cucumbers, Pickled	73	Frosted Fruit	41
Cucumbers, Preserved	85	Fruit Bottling	51
Curaçoa	114	Fruit fit for Preservation	1

Cherries

Red currants

Fig

Bottled Fruit

Garlic

Gooseberries

Fruit, Fresh, to Bottle	54	Greengage Paste	60
Fruits, Frosted	41	Greengage Pulp, Preserved	60
Fruit Jellies	30	Greengages, Bottled	54
Fruit Juice for Ices	65	Greengages in Brandy	58
Fruit for Preserves	1	Greengages Crystallized	42
Fruit Syrups and Juices	63	Greengages, Preserved	42
Fruits, Crystallized	38	Greengages, to Preserve, Dry	42
Fruits in Brandy	57	Greengages Preserved in Syrup	42
Fruits, Glacé	38	Harvey Sauce	92
Garlic Pickle	81	Hawthorn Liqueur	115
Garlic Vinegar	92	Herb Sauce	92
Gherkins, Pickled	74	Home-made Wines	101
Ginger Brandy	115	Horseradish, Pickled	74
Ginger, Green, Preserved	42	Horseradish Vinegar	92
Ginger, Imitation	16	Indian Chutney	71
Ginger Syrup	64	Indian Maize, Pickled	74
Ginger Wine I & II	105/6	Indian Mustard	93
Glacé Fruits	9	Indian Pickle	75
Gooseberries, Bottled	54	Indian Soy	96
Gooseberries, Green, Preserved	42	Jams and Preserves	11
Gooseberry and Currant Jam	16	Jams & Preserves, Best Time to make	10
Gooseberry Chutney	74	Ketchup	93
Gooseberry Jam	16	Ketchup, Anchovy	89
Gooseberry Jelly	33	Ketchup, Cucumber	91
Gooseberry Wine I & II	106/7	Ketchup, Mushroom	94
Grape Jam	17	Ketchup, Pontac	93
Grape Jelly	33	Ketchup, Tomato	97
Grape Marmalade	23	Ketchup, Walnut	98
Grape Wine	107	Leamington Sauce	93
Grated Marmalade	23	Lemon Curd	60
Green Fig Jam	17	Lemon Flip	107
Green Ginger, to Preserve	43	Lemon Gin	115
Green Oranges, to Preserve	44	Lemon Marmalade I, II & III	24
Green Tomato Preserve	17	Lemon Pickle	75
Greengage Jam I & II	17	Lemons, to Preserve Whole	43

Lemon Syrup	64	Mushrooms, to Preserve	86		
Lemon Wine	107	Mustapha Ketchup	94		
Lemons, Fancy	43	Nasturtium Seeds, Pickled	79		
Lemons, Pickled	76	Nectarines, Preserved	44		
Limes, Pickled	76	Noyeau, Imitation I & II	116		
Loganberry Jam	18	Onions and Tomatoes, Pickled	82		
Loquat Jelly	33	Onions, Pickled I & II	79		
Maidenhair Syrup	64	Orange and Rhubarb Jam	20		

Nasturtium

Mango Chutney	72	Orange Brandy	116		
Mango Chutney, Indian	76	Orange Flower Syrup	64		
Mango Pickle, Indian	76	Orange Jelly	33		
Mangoes, Pickled	77	Orange Liqueur	116		
Mangoes, to Preserve	43	Orange Marmalade I & II	24/25		
Marmalades	23	Orange Marmalade with Honey	25		
Marrow Jam	18	Orange Marmalade, Transparent	25		
Medlar Jelly	33	Orange Syrup	64		
Melon Pickle	77	Orange Wine	108		
Melon, Preserved	43	Oranges and Lemons, to Preserve	44		
Melons, Pickled	77	Oranges in Brandy	58		
Mint Vinegar	93	Oranges, Fancy	44		
Mirabelle Jam	18	Oranges, Green, to Preserve	44		
Mirabelle Paste	60	Oranges, to Preserve	45		

Oranges

Mirabelle Plums, Bottled	55	Oysters, Pickled	86		
Mirabelle Plums in Brandy	58	Parsnip Wine	108		
Mirabelle Plums, Preserved/Crystallized	47	Pastes and Curds	59		
Mirabelle Pulp, Preserved	61	Peach and Pineapple Marmalade	26		
Mixed Pickles I, II & III	77/78	Peach Paste	61		
Mogul Plums in Brandy	58	Peach Pickle I & II	80		
Morello Cherry Syrup	64	Peach Pulp, Preserved	61		
Mulberries, Preserved	43	Peaches, Bottled	55		
Mulberry Syrup	64	Peaches, in Brandy	45/58		
Mushroom Ketchup	94	Peaches, Preserved or Crystallized	45		
Mushrooms, Bottled	86	Pears in Brandy	58		
Mushrooms, to Keep Temporarily	86	Pears, Preserved I & II	45		
Mushrooms, Pickled I & II	78/79	Pears, Red, Preserved	46		

Peach

Recipe Index

Pear

Plums

Quince

Pears, Sweet, Pickled	80	Raspberry and Currant Wine	109
Pears, White, Preserved	46	Raspberry Brandy	117
Piccalilli	80	Raspberry Gin	117
Pickles	67	Raspberry Jam	19
Pineapple Chips	46	Raspberry Jelly	35
Pineapple Marmalade	26	Raspberry Syrup	65
Pineapple, Preserved I & II	46	Raspberry Vinegar	95/110
Pineapples, Crystallized	46	Raspberry Wine I & II	110
Piquant Sauce	95	Ratafia	117
Plain Syrup I & II	65	Ratio of Sugar to Jam	4
Plum Jam	18	Reading Sauce	96
Plum Paste	61	Red Cabbage, Pickled	69
Plum Pickle	81	Red Currant Jam	19
Plums, Crystallized	47	Red Currant Jelly I & II	35
Plums, Mirabelle, see Plums Spiced	47	Red Currant Paste	61
Plums, to Preserve	47	Red Currant Wine	104
Plums, to Preserve Dry	47	Red and White Currant Jams	19
Plums, Spiced	47	Rhubarb and Orange Jam	20
Pomegranate Jelly	34	Rhubarb Jam	19
Potting the Jam	6	Rhubarb Marmalade	26
Preserved Fruits	37	Rhubarb Wine	111
Preserves, Dry	38	Rules for Jam-making	8
Prickly Pear Jelly	34	Sauce for Steaks, etc.	96
Prune Jam	19	Shallot Pickle	81
Pumpkin, to Preserve	48	Shallot Sauce	96
Quince and Apple Jam	12	Shallot Vinegar	96
Quince Jelly I, II & III	34	Shrub	117
Quince Marmalade	26	Skimming Jam	4
Quince Paste	61	Sloe Gin	117
Quinces, to Preserve	48	Soy, Indian	96
Quin's Sauce	95	Spanish Onions, Pickled	81
Radish Pods, Pickled	81	Sterilizing Jars	56
Raisin Wine I & II	108/9	Store Sauce	97
Raisin Wine with Cider	109	Storing Jam	7
Raspberries, Bottled	55	Straining for Jelly	6

Strawberries, Bottled	55	Vegetables to Preserve	87	
Strawberries - to Preserve I & II	48/49	Vinegar, Spiced	98	
Strawberry Jam	20	Walnut Ketchup	98	
Strawberry Liqueur	118	Walnuts, Pickled I & II	83	
Strawberry Syrup	65	Water Melon, Preserved	21	
Sugar for Preserving	2	Welsh Nectar	111	
Sugar - to Clarify for Syrup	2	White Currant Jam	19	
'Sugariness'	8	White Currant Jelly	36	
Sweet Pickle	82	Worcester Sauce	99	

Strawberries

Syrup for Preserving — 2
Syrup, Plain — 65
Syrup - to Clarify sugar for — 20
Syrups and Juices — 63
Tamarind Sauce — 97
Tangerine Marmalade — 26
Tarragon Vinegar — 97
Testing Preserves — 5
Tipparee Jelly — 35
Tomato Chow-chow — 82
Tomato Chutney — 82
Tomato Conserve — 87
Tomato Jam — 20
Tomato Ketchup — 97
Tomato Marmalade — 27
Tomato Sauce I & II — 97/8
Tomato Vinegar — 98
Tomatoes, Pickled — 82
Tomatoes and Onions, Pickled — 82
Tomatoes, Preserve of — 21
Unsweetened Fruit Juice for Ices — 65
Utensils for Preserving — 3
Vanilla Liqueur — 118
Vegetable Marrow Jam — 21
Vegetable Marrow Preserve — 21
Vegetable Marrows, Pickled — 83

Tomatoes

Walnuts

Recipe Index   xiii

A Canning Demonstration by Evelyn Dunbar

CHAPTER I

THE ART OF PRESERVING

THE FRUIT

FRUIT intended for preserving should be gathered in the morning, in dry weather, with the morning sun upon them if possible; they then have their fullest flavour, and keep in good condition longer than when gathered at any other time. Until fruit can be used, it should be placed in a refrigerator or in the dairy. Fruit gathered in wet or foggy weather will soon mildew, and be of no service for preserves unless it is used immediately and very thoroughly boiled, when it may be made into preserve or jam that will keep, though of course of inferior quality. There is no mistake more common than to suppose that any half ripe or over-ripe fruit is good enough for jam.

Preparing the Fruit

The fruit should be quite sound and not over-ripe, and must be carefully wiped and cleaned. Each recipe gives precise details, showing how the specific fruit must be prepared.

SUGAR FOR PRESERVING

Sugar Loaf Box

Of the various kinds of sugar in common use, the white refined lump is generally sold for preserving, and, indeed, is the only kind admissible for the more delicate kinds of preserves. Coarse brown sugar conceals the flavour of fruit, and the whiter moist sugar has little sweetening power. Crystallized Demerara makes good preserves, is very sweet, seldom adulterated, and is less expensive than lump sugar, so that for common preserves it is very suitable. To help to neutralize the acidity of fruit, and yet use less sugar, successful experiments have been made by using only 8 oz. of sugar to the pound of soft fruit, such as strawberries, to this a level teaspoonful of salt is added. By this means the flavour of the fruit is better retained. The sugar should be warmed before use.

SYRUP FOR PRESERVING

Having secured the most important contributions to the manufacture of preserves, the fruit and the sugar, the next consideration is the preparation of the syrup in which the fruit is to be suspended; and this requires much care. In the confectioner's art there is a great nicety in proportioning the degree of concentration of the syrup very exactly to each particular case; this they know by signs, and express it in certain technical terms. But to distinguish these properly requires very great attention and considerable experience. The principal thing to be acquainted with is the fact that, in proportion as the syrup is longer boiled, the water contained in it will become evaporated, and the consistency of the syrup thickened. Care must be taken in the management of the fire, that the syrup does not boil over, and that the boiling is not carried to such an extent as to burn the sugar. If the preserving-pan is greased with good salad oil or butter, the jam will not be likely to burn. A solution of sugar prepared by dissolving 2 parts of double-refined sugar in 1 of water, and boiling this a little, affords a syrup of the right degree of strength, which neither ferments nor crystallizes. This appears to be the degree called **small** or **large thread** by the confectioners (215°-217°F.). The syrup employed should sometimes be clarified, which is done in the following manner: dissolve 2 lb. of loaf sugar in 1 pint of water; add to this solution the white of an egg, and beat it well. Put the preserving-pan upon the fire with the solution, stir it with a wooden spatula, and, when it begins to swell and boil up, throw in some cold water to damp the boiling, for, as it rises suddenly, should it boil over it would take fire, being of a very inflammable nature. Let it boil up again; then take it off, and remove carefully the scum that has risen. Boil the solution again, throw in a little more cold water, remove the scum, and so on for three or four times successively, then strain it. It is sufficiently boiled when some taken up in a spoon pours out like oil.

Although sugar passes so easily into the state of fermentation, yet it will not ferment at all if the quantity be sufficient to constitute a very strong syrup; hence, syrups are used to preserve fruits and other vegetable substances from the changes they would undergo if left to themselves.

FRUIT FIT FOR PRESERVATION IN SYRUP

The fruits that are the most fit for preservation in syrup are apricots, peaches, nectarines, apples, greengages, plums of all kinds, and pears. As an example, take some apricots, not too ripe, make a small slit at the stem end, withdraw the stone, simmer them in water until about half-cooked, and afterwards throw them into cold water. When they have cooled, take them out and drain them. Put the apricots into the preserving-pan with sufficient syrup to cover them; boil up three or four times, and then skim well; remove them from the fire, pour them into an earthen pan, and let them cool till next day. Boil them up three days successively, skimming each time, and they will soon be finished and in a state fit to be put into pots for use. After each boiling the consistency of the syrup should be noted; if too thin, it will bear additional boiling; if too thick, it may be lowered with more syrup of the usual standard. The reason why the fruit is emptied out of the preserving-pan into an earthen pan is, that the acid of the fruit acts upon the copper of which the preserving-pans are usually made. From this example the process of preserving fruits by syrup will be easily comprehended.

JAMS AND MARMALADES

Marmalades and jams differ little from each other: they are preserves of half liquid consistency, made by boiling the pulp of fruits, and sometimes part of the rinds, with sugar. The term marmalade is applied to those confitures which are composed of the firmer fruits, as pineapples or the rinds of oranges; whereas jams are made of the more juicy berries, such as strawberries, raspberries, currants, mulberries, etc. Jams require the same care and attention in the boiling as marmalade; the slightest degree of burning communicates a disagreeable empyreumatic taste, and if jams are not boiled properly they will not keep.

UTENSILS NECESSARY FOR PRESERVING

To make marmalades and jams successfully a properly constructed preserving-pan or maslin-kettle is necessary. Formerly these were composed of solid brass or copper, and formed one of the careful housewife's most cherished possessions. Enamelled iron ones may now be obtained at a comparatively trifling cost, but the objection to their use is that the syrup boils over more quickly than in a preserving pan made of copper or brass, and moreover it is more apt to burn and stick to the bottom of the pan. A long wooden spoon or stick is necessary. The end to be attained is to boil the juice of the fruit to such a consistency that it will neither ferment nor mildew. Some persons add a little water, others put only the fruit in with the sugar.

RATIO OF SUGAR TO JAM

From ¾ of a lb. to 1 lb. of sugar for each lb. of fruit is the usual amount, but ½ a lb. is sometimes enough to preserve the fruit, and if this quantity is sufficient no more should be used, as jam is often unpleasantly sweet with very little flavour of the fruit left. The methods employed vary considerably; sometimes the fruit is boiled a long time and slowly, and the sugar added towards the end of the process; but more frequently the sugar is boiled first with a little water, and the fruit added afterwards and boiled from 20 to 60 minutes.

The latter method is commonly employed in factories where time is money, and it certainly preserves the shape, colour, and flavour of the fruit better than the former, which, however, has advantages for some fruits that require long stewing, and for those persons who find it difficult, with the means at their disposal, to make the jam boil as thoroughly and completely as it readily does in the manufacturer's pans, heated to the exact temperature required.

BOILING THE PRESERVE

All sorts of jam should be boiled rapidly, as quick cooking improves both the flavour and colour of the jam. Jams made from juicy fruits, such as raspberries and strawberries, will require from 55 to 60 minutes to cook, while most of the other jams will only take about 45 minutes. The times stated in the various recipes are reckoned from when the jam actually commences to boil. When the fruit is very ripe, little or no water is required, but the full quantity of sugar must be added.

SKIMMING THE JAM

During the process of boiling the jam should be frequently skimmed, otherwise it will not be beautifully clear when finished. A long-handled wooden spoon should be used and the scum thus removed should not be wasted. Place it in a clean basin and stand the basin in a cool cupboard until the scum is quite cold, carefully remove a thin top layer and the remainder will be found excellent for immediate use. It will not keep very long.

Skimming the Jam

The jam should be skimmed frequently. Allow the jar of scum which has been taken from the jam to stand for about 24 hours; remove the top layer and the remainder will be quite good to eat.

TESTING THE PRESERVE

The jam is sufficiently cooked when a little dropped on to a clean plate sets as soon as it is cold. Otherwise, boil a little longer and test again. Some fruits may be kept whole by straining them from the syrup as soon as they are sufficiently cooked, the syrup then being boiled rapidly until it forms a jelly when tested, and the fruit subsequently replaced in it for a final gentle boil.

Testing the Jam

The jam is sufficiently cooked when a little of it jellies if dropped on to a cold plate.

STRAINING FOR JELLY

When making jelly great care must be taken that the syrup and fruit juice is not boiled too much, otherwise the colour will be entirely spoiled and the liquid will become thick and ropy like treacle. When the syrup and fruit juice has been sufficiently boiled it must be passed through a fine sieve or a jelly bag to clear. An excellent substitute for sieve or jelly bag, if these are not available, may be improvised by turning a chair upside down and tying a clean piece of rather coarse linen to the legs of the chair. Place a large bowl underneath and pour a basin of boiling water through the linen. Remove the bowl directly the water has run through the linen and substitute a clean basin, then pour the liquid to be strained gently through the strainer. Repeat this process two or three times, if necessary, until the jelly is perfectly clear. A basin of hot water is sometimes stood in the linen to hasten the straining, but the liquid should not otherwise be interfered with or it will be rendered cloudy. Always scald a jelly bag before using it.

Fruits such as apples, gooseberries, quinces, Seville oranges, red currants and those containing a large amount of pectin or vegetable jelly are most suitable for making jelly.

STERILIZING THE JARS

Before the hot jam is placed into the jars or pots, the latter should be carefully sterilized by being thoroughly cleansed, well dried and, if possible, stood in the oven until fairly hot. Another method of sterilization is to fill the jars or pots with sulphur fumes [not recommended today!], the pots being then turned upside down. Whichever method is employed, the jars or pots should be used immediately, either hot or as soon as the sulphur fumes have been allowed to escape. When using earthenware jars it is always advisable to have one glass jar in each batch. It will then be possible to see how the jam is keeping.

COVERING THE POTS OR BOTTLES

As soon as the jam is ready the jars or pots should be filled and at once covered and fastened down before the escaping steam has lost its power to exclude the air. Cover the jars or pots with vegetable parchment damped in cold water, and fasten down securely. Thin paper dipped in milk may be substituted for the parchment or a piece of damp bladder can be stretched over the top, the jam being first covered with a small piece of thin white paper. Bladder is much to be preferred for covering all kinds of pickles.

When bottling fruit and vegetables it is best to use jars fitted with vacuum or screw-top air-tight lids - preferably of glass. If, however, parchment or butter paper is to be employed

as a covering, it is wise to use a layer of oil, fat, or brine over the preserve as an additional guard against the penetration of air. Any of the following methods will be found suitable:-
1. Carefully fit a piece of butter paper over the top of the preserve and on this pour a strong solution of salt brine.
2. Over the preserve pour a thin layer of clarified mutton fat, about one inch in thickness. Be careful not to move the jar until the fat has set and formed a hard protecting surface. If on cooling it is noticed that the fat has contracted away from the sides of the jar, pour over a second layer of melted fat which will run down the edges of the previous layer and prevent penetration of the air. Cover as in (1). A covering of about a ¼ of an inch of clarified butter may be substituted for the mutton fat, if preferred.
3. Over the hot preserve pour a tablespoonful of warm salad oil. Cover immediately as in (1). Store where the oil will not be so shaken as to come into contact with the paper top, which, should this happen, would become porous and admit the air.

Covering the Pots

Superfluous moisture should be wiped off the vegetable parchment or milk-paper, which is then tied down securely, while damp; it will be quite tight when dry.

STORING JAM

The pots in which the jam is put must be perfectly dry, and the cupboard in which they stand neither so warm that the jam ferments, nor damp so that it becomes mouldy. The housekeeper will do well to remember that mould is a plant sowing itself by multitudes of seeds, so small that they penetrate the tiniest crack. It spreads, therefore, readily from one thing to another, and may sometimes lurk unsuspected on the shelves of a cupboard that is not well cleansed and aired. Formerly jam was allowed to become quite cold before being covered, under the erroneous belief that the steam arising from it would, if confined, produce mould. Now jams, jellies, and marmalades of every description are covered as speedily as possible, before the escaping steam loses its power to exclude the air.

"SUGARINESS" AND FERMENTATION

Should the preserve show signs of fermentation, it must all be returned as quickly as possible, with a little additional sugar, to the preserving-pan. The pulp should now be boiled and well skimmed, and the addition of a little glycerine, when boiling, will usually prevent further fermentation taking place. If the jam is very stiff, a little water should be added at the outset.

If the jam or jelly in the pot becomes "sugary" the pot should be placed in a pan of cold water in the oven, and the water boiled until the jelly or jam melts. When the preserve has again cooled, it will be found that it is quite clear and free from grain or "sugariness."

RULES ESSENTIAL TO SUCCESSFUL JAM-MAKING

1. Scrupulous cleanliness in all details.
2. Absolutely sound, fresh, ripe and dry fruit only should be used.
3. Only the best cane sugar should be used, allowing from ¾ - to 1 lb. of sugar to every lb. of fruit.
4. Keep the jam boiling and stir and skim frequently.
5. Boil the jam until it sets quickly when a little is tested on a cold plate.
6. The jars or pots for storing the jam must be scrupulously clean and dry.
7. Cover the jars or pots immediately before the escaping steam loses its power to exclude air.
8. Store the pots in a cool, dry place.

BOTTLING FRUIT AND VEGETABLES

This is one of the most simple and easy methods of preserving fruit and vegetables, especially when one possesses a proper bottling outfit, although this is by no means essential. Full instructions as to the various methods of bottling fruit and vegetables will be found in the introduction to Chapter VI.

DRYING FRUIT AND VEGETABLES

This, also, is a very easy process, the only necessary equipment being some drying trays. It may be necessary to wipe over stone fruit, which is afterwards cut open or else cut in half so that the stones may be removed. Cherries, owing to the amount of juice they lose in the process, are better left unstoned. Stoned fruit should be placed on the drying tray cut side uppermost and reversed when that side is thoroughly dried.

Such fruits as apples and pears should be peeled thinly, cored and cut into small quarters or rings. Pears can also be cut into slices or halves. A plated knife should always be used when thus preparing fruit.

The fruit is usually dried in the oven on trays, but fruit rings may be suspended on sticks so cut as to fit the ledges which support the oven shelves; the oven door must be kept open to allow the air to circulate freely, or the fruits will be "baked" instead of being dried. The temperatures for drying vary between 110° F. and 150° F.; a higher temperature should never be used; a lower one may equally well be employed, but the process will naturally be lengthened.

When the preserves are properly dried they should be quite dry and shrivelled in appearance. Cut away a small section of the fruit and if the interior appears very moist further drying is necessary. Dried root vegetables, plums and such fruits should not be brittle but quite pliable. Any fruits that have been preserved in syrup may be converted into dry preserves, by first draining them from the syrup and then drying them on a stove or in a very moderate oven, adding to them a quantity of fine powdered loaf sugar. They should be dried on a sieve or tray and turned every 6 or 8 hours, fresh powdered sugar being sifted over them each time they are turned.

CRYSTALLIZED AND CANDIED OR GLACÉ FRUITS

Fruit that is to be preserved in either of these forms should be carefully selected and only perfectly sound, ripe and dry fruit must be used. It should first be boiled in syrup. Immediately on its removal from the syrup, fruit to be crystallized must be rolled in finely crushed loaf sugar and afterwards dried. Fruit to be candied or iced is dried before the fire or in a cool oven, the syrup in which it was cooked being meanwhile boiled to the "large blow" degree (233° F.). When the syrup has cooled a little the fruit should be dipped into it until thoroughly coated and then dried.

HOME-MADE WINES, LIQUEURS, ETC.

When fruit is sufficiently cheap and plentiful for the housewife to undertake the making of home-made jams and marmalades and the preserving and bottling of fruit, the making and storing of home-made wines, etc., will invariably enter also into her activities. Full instructions will be found in Chapters XIII and XIV, but a few general remarks may not be out of place here.

A common mistake is to use a large cask, which the wine does not fill. When the wine is set to ferment, stand the cask, which must not be too big, in a fairly warm place, and fill it, reserving a small quantity of the wine to fill up with as fermentation takes place. The bung must be left out until all suspicion of hissing ceases. As soon as this is so, insert the bung and drive in the vent peg. The latter, however, must be left loose and not tightened for several days yet. Be very careful in drawing the wine off not to disturb the sediment at the bottom of the cask or the wine will be thick in the bottles. Cork securely and seal with bottling wax or wire according to the nature of the wine.

BEST TIME TO MAKE JAMS AND PRESERVES

In June and July currants, raspberries, strawberries, gooseberries, and other summer fruits should be preserved and jams and jellies made.

In the autumn plums, damsons, blackberries, cranberries and many other fruits should be bottled and preserved and jams and jellies made. Apples and pears for winter use should be gathered in and carefully stored in a dry place. The fruit should be frequently looked over, and any showing symptoms of decay removed. Filberts, cob nuts and walnuts should be preserved in sand and salt.

The following table shows when the various fruits are in season and when they are at their best and cheapest:-

Gooseberries

Fruit.	In Season.	Best and Cheapest.
Apples	All the year	Oct. to Dec.
Apricots	June to Dec.	August
Bananas	All the year	—
Blackberries	Sept. to Oct.	September
Bullaces	Autumn	October
Cherries	June to Aug.	July
Cranberries	Nov. to Jan.	December
Currants	July to Sept.	August
Damsons	Sept. to Oct.	October
Figs (green)	July to Sept.	August
Gooseberries	,,	,,
,, (Green)	May to July	June
Grapes (Foreign)	All the year	Autumn
,, (Hothouse)	Sept. to Nov.	October
Grape Fruit	All the year	Autumn
Greengages	Aug. and Sept.	August
Lemons	All the year	—
Medlars	Oct. to Jan.	Oct. to Nov.
Melons	June to Nov.	October
Nectarines	Sept. and Oct.	,,
Oranges	All the year	Winter
Peaches	Sept. and Oct.	October
Pears	Sept. to March	Oct. and Nov.
Pineapples	All the year	Summer months
Plums	Aug. to Oct.	Sept. and Oct.
Pumpkins	Sept. to Oct.	October
Quinces	Sept. and Oct.	,,
Raspberries	June to Sept.	July
Rhubarb	Jan. to May	March and April
Strawberries	June to Sept.	July

CHAPTER II

RECIPES FOR JAMS AND PRESERVES

APPLE AND BLACKBERRY JAM

Have ready 4 lb. of apples, 2 lb. of blackberries and 4½ lb. of preserving sugar.

Pick the blackberries, put them into a stew-jar with 1 lb. of sugar, and let them remain thus for at least 12 hours. When ready, place the jar on the stove or in a cool oven, and stew gently until the juice is extracted. Pare, core and cut the apples into thick slices. Put them into a preserving-pan, strain in the juice, add the rest of the sugar, and boil gently from 45 to 50 minutes. Pour into jars, cover closely, and store in a dry, cool place.

APPLE GINGER

Procure 5 lb. of sour apples, 4 lb. of loaf sugar, 2 oz. of whole ginger, ¼ of a teaspoonful of cayenne, 3 lemons and 1 pint of cold water.

Peel, core, and cut the apples into quarters. Dissolve 2 lb. of sugar in 1 pint of water, bring slowly to boiling-point, skim well, and simmer for 8 or 10 minutes. Pour the syrup over the prepared apples, cover, and let it remain thus for 48 hours. When ready, drain off the syrup into a stewpan, add the remaining 2 lb. of sugar, the strained juice, and finely grated rinds of the lemons, the ginger bruised and tied in fine muslin, and the cayenne. When boiling, add the apples, simmer very gently until they are soft, but not broken, then turn into jars. Cover with ready-prepared paper, or paper brushed over with white of egg, and fasten securely. Store the jars away in a cool, dry place until required for use.

APPLE GINGER II

Take 2 lb. of sour apples, 2 lb. of loaf sugar, ½ an oz. of extract of ginger and 1½ pints of water.

Make a syrup of the sugar and water, as directed in the preceding recipe. Meanwhile peel, core, and cut each apple into 8 sections, add them with the extract of ginger to the syrup, and simmer gently until soft, but not broken. Turn into jars, cover as directed in the preceding recipe, and store in a cool, dry place.

Quince

APPLE JAM

To each lb. of fruit, weighed after being pared, cored and sliced, allow ¾ of a lb. of preserving sugar, the finely-grated rind of 1 lemon and the juice of ½ a lemon.

Choose firm, sound apples of the same kind; peel, core, and cut them into thick slices. Barely cover the bottom of a large stew-jar with cold water, add a good layer of sliced apples, cover thickly with sugar, and sprinkle with lemon-rind and lemon-juice. Repeat until all the materials are used, cover the jar closely, place it on the stove or in a moderate oven, in a tin half-full of boiling water, and stew gently until the apples are tender. If the preparation appears rather dry it may at once be put into the pots; if not, the lid must be removed, the stew-jar taken out of the water and placed on the stove, and the contents boiled and stirred until most of the moisture has evaporated.

APPLE JAM II

Take 4 lb. of sour apples, 3 lb. of preserving sugar, the finely-grated rind and juice of 2 lemons, 1 saltspoonful [¼ of a teaspoon] of ground cinnamon and ¼ of a pint of cold water.

Pare, core and cut the apples into thick slices. Place them in a preserving-pan, add the sugar, lemon-rind and juice, cinnamon and water, and cook gently until reduced to a pulp. During the first part of the process stir occasionally, but towards the end, when the greater part of the moisture has evaporated, stir more frequently to prevent the preparation sticking to the bottom of the pan. Pour into jars, cover closely, and store in a cool, dry place. This jam will not keep so long as that made according to the preceding recipe.

APPLE AND QUINCE JAM

Pare and core an equal number of good apples and quinces. Cut them in pieces, and put them into a pan with a gill [¼ of a pint] of water to each pound. Boil them until they are reduced to a pulp, pass them through a sieve, and add ¾ of a lb. of cane sugar to each lb. of pulp. Put the jam over a clear fire, and stir until it is thick and becomes jellied. Remove from the fire, and put into dry, clean jars.

APRICOT JAM

Take 3 lb. of ripe apricots, pass them through a hair sieve, and add 1 lb. of cane sugar to 1 lb. of pulp. Put them in a pan over a clear fire, and stir them well as they boil with ½ a pint of water. After 20 to 30 minutes' boiling remove them from the fire, add the kernels of the apricots, and then put the jam into clean, dry pots. Cover the pots with paper soaked in brandy and parchment.

APRICOT JAM OR MARMALADE

Skin some firm, ripe apricots carefully, break them in halves and remove the stones. Weigh the fruit, and allow an equal amount of fine preserving sugar. Pile the apricots on a large dish, sprinkle each layer with sugar, let them stand for 12 hours, and meanwhile remove the kernels from the stones and blanch them. When ready, place the fruit, sugar and kernels in a preserving-pan, simmer very gently, skimming meanwhile, and as the pieces of apricot become clear remove them from the syrup and place them at once in the pots. Pour on the syrup and kernels, cover with pieces of paper dipped in salad-oil, and stretch over the tops of the jars tissue paper brushed over with white of egg. When dry, the cover will be perfectly hard and air-tight.

BANANA JAM

Take 6 lb. bananas, 5 lb. loaf sugar, 2 lb. juicy pears and the juice of 3 lemons.

Cut the peeled bananas into small dice and weigh them. Put into the preserving-pan the lemon-juice, the pears (peeled and cut up) and 1 lb. of sugar. When boiling put in gradually the bananas and remainder of sugar, stir gently, skim well, and boil for 1 hour. Pour into hot jars and cover.

BARBERRY JAM

Put equal quantities of barberries and preserving sugar into a preserving-pan and bring slowly to boiling-point. Boil gently for about 15 or 20 minutes, skimming well and stirring frequently, pour into small pots, cover closely, and store in a cool, dry place.

Barberries

BEETROOT AND CARROT JAM (*See* Carrot and Beetroot Jam)

BLACKBERRY JAM

Boil some blackberries and half their weight in sugar together for 40 minutes. Cover closely, and keep in a dry, cool place. The jam will be less insipid if a little lemon-juice is added.

BLACKBERRY AND APPLE JAM (*See* Apple and Blackberry Jam)

BLACK-CURRANT JAM

To each lb. of fruit allow 1 lb. of loaf sugar, and ¼ of a pint of water.

Remove the fruit, which should be ripe and perfectly dry, from the stalks, put it into a preserving-pan with the water, bring to boiling-point, and simmer gently for 20 minutes.

Recipes for Jams and Preserves

Add the sugar and boil for about half an hour from the time the jam re-boils, or until a little almost immediately sets when tested on a cold plate. Towards the end of the process the jam must be stirred almost continuously to prevent it boiling over or sticking to the bottom of the pan. Pour into pots, cover closely, and store in a cool, dry place, until required.

BLACK-CURRANT JAM II

Have ready 8 lb. of black currants, 4 lb. of rhubarb and 8 lb. of sugar.

Remove the stalks, pick out the best and finest fruit, place about 6 lb. of it on a large dish between layers of sugar, and let it remain for 24 hours. Put the remainder of the currants into a large jar, add the rhubarb previously peeled and cut into short lengths, and cook in a slow oven or in a saucepan of boiling water until all the juice is extracted. Of this juice take not less than 1½ pints and not more than 2 pints, put it into a large earthenware pan or bowl, add the fruit and sugar, and let the whole stand for 24 hours longer. At the end of this time strain the juice into a preserving-pan, bring to boiling-point, add more sugar if necessary, and boil for about 10 minutes. Now add the fruit, boil gently for 20 minutes, skimming when necessary, then turn the jam into pots, cover closely, and store in a cool, dry place until required.

CARROT AND BEETROOT JAM

Procure equal weights of carrots and beetroot.

Wash the beetroot, scrape the carrots, and boil them separately until tender. Pass through a coarse sieve, measure the puree, and to each pint allow 12 oz. of sugar and the juice of 2 lemons. Place the whole in a preserving-pan, boil gently for half an hour, and turn the preparation into pots. If intended to be kept some time, a glass of brandy should be added to each pint of jam before putting it into the pot. Keep closely covered in a dry, cool place.

CARROT JAM

Wash and scrape the carrots, which must be nice and young, cut each one into 3 or 4 pieces, place them in a preserving-pan with barely sufficient water to cover them, and simmer gently till tender. Drain well, pass through a fine sieve, weigh the pulp, and to each lb. allow 1 lb. of preserving sugar, the strained juice of 2 lemons, and grated rind of 1 lemon, 6 chopped bitter almonds, 2 tablespoonfuls of brandy. Replace the pulp in the preserving-pan with the preserving sugar. Bring slowly to boiling-point, boil for about 5 minutes, stirring and skimming frequently. When cool, add the almonds, brandy, lemon-juice and rind, turn into pots, cover closely, and store in a cool, dry place. If the brandy be omitted the jam will not keep.

Carrot

CARROT JAM (Imitation Apricot)

Take equal weights of carrots and sugar. To each lb. of carrots allow 1½ tablespoonfuls of brandy, the juice of 2 lemons, the thin rind of 1 lemon and 12 sweet almonds blanched and quartered.

Scrape and slice the carrots, barely cover them with cold water, simmer slowly until tender, then drain well and pass them through a fine sieve. Replace in the pan, add the sugar, almonds and lemon-juice, boil up, simmer gently for 15 minutes, and stir in the brandy. Turn into pots, cover with bladder, and store in a dry, cool place. Unless the brandy is added the jam will not keep.

CHERRY JAM

Have ready some sound, ripe cooking cherries, an equal quantity of preserving sugar and to each lb. of fruit allow ¼ of a pint of red-currant juice or water, or the two mixed in any proportions convenient.

Remove the stones, keeping the cherries as whole as possible, and preserve the kernels. Put the red-currant juice or water into a preserving-pan with the sugar, and boil to a syrup. Add the cherries and kernels, and simmer gently until the cherries are tender, but not broken, and the juice jellies almost immediately when a little is poured on a cold plate. Pour into jars, cover with paper dipped in brandy, and stretch over the top tissue paper brushed over with white of egg. Store in a cool, dry place.

CURRANT AND RASPBERRY JAM (*See* Raspberry Jam)

DAMSON JAM

To each lb. of damsons allow from ¾ to 1 lb. of preserving sugar, according to taste.

Remove the stalks, put the fruit and sugar into a preserving-pan, let it stand by the side of the fire until some of the juice is extracted, then bring slowly to boiling-point, occasionally stirring meanwhile. Boil gently for about 45 minutes, or until the syrup, when tested on a cold plate, stiffens readily. Pour into pots. Cover with paper brushed over with white of egg.

DAMSON JAM II

To each lb. of fruit allow 1 lb. of sugar.

Remove the stalks, put the fruit into a preserving-pan, let it stand by the side of the fire until a little of the juice is extracted, then boil them for half an hour. Now add the sugar gradually, and boil for 20 minutes longer, reckoning from the time the jam re-boils. It must

Damsons

Fig

be frequently stirred, and, if preferred, some or all the stones may be removed before turning the jam into the pots. Cover closely with paper brushed over with white of egg.

FIG JAM (*See* Green Fig Jam)

GINGER (Imitation)

Take 24 sticks of well-grown rhubarb, or a corresponding quantity of stalks of lettuce going to seed.

Remove the outside stringy part, and cut the stalks into 2-inch lengths. Put them into a preserving-pan with 4 pints of cold water, 1 lb. of preserving sugar, and 1 heaped tablespoonful of ground ginger. Bring slowly to boiling-point, simmer for about 20 minutes, then turn the whole into an earthenware vessel. On the following day drain the juice into the preserving-pan, when boiling, add the stalks and simmer gently for about ½ an hour. Repeat this process on the two following days, then drain the stalks and weigh them. To each lb. allow 1½ oz. of ground ginger, 1 lb. of loaf sugar, and 1½ pints of cold water. Boil these together to the "large thread" degree (217° F.), and pour the syrup over the stalks. When cold, put the preparation into jars, cover closely, and store in a cool, dry place for about 3 weeks, when it will be ready for use.

GOOSEBERRY AND CURRANT JAM

Have ready 6 lb. of red hairy gooseberries, 4 lb. of preserving sugar and ½ a pint of currant juice. (See Red Currant Jelly.)

Head and tail the gooseberries, put them into a preserving--pan, and allow them to stand by the side of the fire until some of the juice is extracted. Bring to boiling-point; when the gooseberries have boiled for 10 minutes add the sugar gradually, put in the red-currant juice, and boil until the jam sets when tested on a cold plate. The scum must be removed as it rises, and the jam should be well stirred towards the end of the boiling process. When ready pour into pots, cover closely and store in a cool, dry place.

GOOSEBERRY JAM

To each lb. of gooseberries allow 1 lb. of preserving sugar and ½ a pint of cold water.

Top and tail the gooseberries. Dissolve the sugar in the cold water, boil up, simmer for about 15 minutes, and remove the scum as it rises. Now put in the fruit, boil gently from 35 to 40 minutes, or until the jam sets readily when tested on a cold plate. Pour into pots, cover with paper brushed over on both sides with white of egg, and store in a cool, dry place.

GRAPE JAM

Procure some firm, sound, unripe grapes, and to each lb. allow ½ a lb. of preserving sugar.

Place the fruit and sugar in layers in a preserving-pan, allow it to stand by the side of the fire until the whole mass is thoroughly hot and some of the juice is extracted, then bring slowly to boiling-point. Boil until the juice sets quickly when tested on a cold plate, pour into small pots, cover closely, and keep in a cool, dry place.

Note: In France, about ¼ of a lb. of apples are added to each lb. of grapes.

GREEN FIG JAM

To 2 lb. of figs allow 1½ lb. of sugar, ½ a pint of water and the juice of 1 lemon.

Boil the water, sugar, and lemon-juice together for 10 minutes, then wipe and slice the fruit, and add it to the syrup. Boil gently for about 1 hour, or until a little of the syrup poured on to a cold plate quickly jellies. Turn into pots, cover and store in a dry place.

GREENGAGE JAM

To each lb. of firm, sound greengages, allow ¾ of a lb. of preserving sugar.

Remove the stalks and stones, crack a few of the latter, and put the kernels aside. Cover the bottom of a preserving-pan to the depth of ½ an inch with cold water, put in the fruit and kernels, bring slowly to boiling-point, and boil gently for about 15 minutes. Meanwhile, the sugar should have been placed in the oven in a deep tin or dish, and allowed to become thoroughly hot. It may now be added gradually to the fruit, and the boiling must be continued until the jam sets quickly when tested on a cold plate. Pour into pots, cover with paper brushed over with white of egg, and store in a cool, dry place.

GREENGAGE JAM II

Take 3 lb. of ripe greengages, extract the stones, and add 2½ lb. of cane sugar. Put them over a clear fire, boil for 20 to 30 minutes, remove them from the fire, add the kernels, and finish as for Apricot Jam.

GREEN TOMATO PRESERVE

Have ready 6 lb. of green tomatoes, 8 lb. of preserving sugar, 4 lemons, 2½ doz. peach leaves, 3 pieces of ginger and 3 table-spoonfuls of brandy.

Cover the tomatoes with water, put in the peach leaves, and boil very gently until the tomatoes are quite soft but unbroken. Drain the water into another pan, add to it the sugar, and boil to a syrup. Strain, when cold replace in the pan, put in the thinly-pared lemon-rind

Grapes

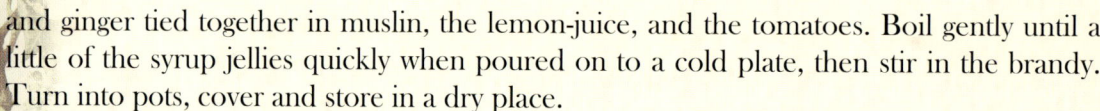

Loganberries

and ginger tied together in muslin, the lemon-juice, and the tomatoes. Boil gently until a little of the syrup jellies quickly when poured on to a cold plate, then stir in the brandy. Turn into pots, cover and store in a dry place.

LOGANBERRY JAM

Prepare 3 lb. loganberries, 1 lb. raspberries, or blackberries or red currants, 4 lb. preserving sugar, and place them in a preserving-pan, add 1 pint water and cook slowly, skimming occasionally, until the fruit is tender and sets if a little is put out on to a cold plate.

If preferred the loganberries may first be partly cooked in the water and then boiled with the other ingredients for about ½ hour. In either case, as soon as the jam is sufficiently cooked, pour it into clean dry jars, cover, tie down and store in a cool place.

MARROW JAM

Peel and slice the vegetable marrow, and remove all the seeds. To every pound of marrow allow ¾ of a lb. of good preserving sugar, which must be placed in alternate layers with the shred marrow, and allowed to remain undisturbed for not less than 12 hours. When ready, boil gently for about an hour, then add a teaspoonful of ginger to each 4 lb. of marrow, stir until well mixed, and turn into pots or glass jars; cover with parchment paper covers, and store in a dry place.

MIRABELLE JAM

Take 3 lb. of ripe mirabelle plums, extract the stones, add 2½ lb. of cane sugar, and put them on a clear fire. Boil for about 25 minutes, then remove them from the fire, put them into dry jars, covering down with brandy paper and parchment.

ORANGE AND RHUBARB JAM (*See* Rhubarb and Orange Jam)

PLUM JAM

To each lb. of plums allow from 12 to 16 oz. of preserving sugar, according to the degree of sweetness required, and the amount of acidity contained in the plums. Divide the plums, take out the stones, or, if preferred, cut them across, and remove the stones as they rise in the pan. Pile the fruit on a large dish with the sugar spread thickly between each layer, allow them to remain thus until the following day, then put the whole into a preserving-pan, and heat slowly by the side of the fire, stirring occasionally meanwhile. Boil gently until the jam sets quickly when tested on a cold plate, then turn it into pots, cover closely, and keep it in a cool, dry place.

PRUNE JAM

Wash and soak 2 lb. of prunes overnight in about 2½ pints of cold water and boil in a clean pan for about ½ an hour. Remove the prunes and stone them. Put the liquid in a preserving-pan with the finely grated rind and juice of 2 lemons and 1¾ lb. of sugar, and boil until a thick syrup is obtained. Next add the prunes and allow them to cook slowly until quite tender. When sufficiently boiled, the jam when tested on a cold plate should set. Pour into clean dry pots, cover, tie down and store in a cool place. If liked, some of the stones of the prunes may be cracked and the kernels peeled and mixed with the jam.

RASPBERRY JAM

To every lb. of raspberries allow 1 lb. of sugar and ½ a pint of red-currant juice.

Let the fruit for this preserve be gathered in fine weather, and used as soon after it is picked as possible. Take off the stalks, put the raspberries into a preserving-pan, break them well with a wooden spoon, and let them boil for about ¼ of an hour, keeping them well stirred. Add the currant-juice and sugar, and boil again for ½ an hour. Skim the jam well after the sugar is added, or the preserve will not be clear. The addition of the currant-juice is a very great improvement to this preserve, as it gives it the piquant taste which the flavour of the raspberries seems to require.

RED-CURRANT JAM

Remove the stalks from the currants, put the fruit into a preserving-pan, and to each lb. allow ¾ of a lb. of preserving sugar. Stir occasionally until the fruit is nearly boiling, and afterwards almost continuously. Boil gently for about 40 minutes, or until a little will set when poured on to a cold plate. Turn into pots, cover closely, and store in a cool dry place.

RED AND WHITE CURRANT JAMS

Pick the currants, put them in a preserving-pan over a clear fire, and stir until mashed. Then pass them through a sieve, add 1 lb. of cane sugar to an equal weight of pulp, and finish as for Apricot Jam.

RHUBARB JAM

To each lb. of rhubarb allow 1 lb. of preserving sugar, ½ a teaspoonful of ground ginger, and the finely-grated rind of ½ a lemon.

Remove the outer stringy part of the rhubarb, cut it into short lengths, and weigh it. Put it into a preserving-pan with sugar, ginger, and lemon-rind in the above proportions, place

Red, white and black-currants

the pan by the side of the fire, and let the contents come very slowly to boiling-point, stirring occasionally meanwhile. Boil until the jam sets quickly when tested on a cold plate. Pour it into pots, cover closely, and store.

RHUBARB AND ORANGE JAM

Take 1 quart of finely-cut rhubarb, 6 oranges and 1½ lb. of preserving sugar.

Cut the rinds of the oranges into sections, remove them and scrape off as much of the white pith as possible. Free the pulp from fibrous skin and pips, put it into a preserving-pan, with the sugar, rhubarb and orange-rinds, previously finely-shredded. Bring slowly to boiling-point, skim well, and boil until the jam stiffens when tested on a cold plate. Cover closely, and store in a cool, dry place.

STRAWBERRY JAM

To each lb. of strawberries allow 12 to 16 oz. of preserving sugar.

Remove the stalks from the fruit, put it into a preserving-pan, covering each layer thickly with sugar. Place the pan by the side of the fire, bring the contents slowly to boiling-point, and stir occasionally. Skim well, boil gently until the jam sets when tested on a cold plate, taking care in stirring to keep the fruit as whole as possible. Pour into pots, cover with paper brushed over on both sides with white of egg, and keep in a cool, dry place.

SYRUP (To Clarify Sugar for)

To 2 lb. of loaf sugar allow 1 pint of water and the white of 1 egg.

Put the sugar, white of egg and water into a stewpan; when the sugar is dissolved place the stewpan by the side of the fire, and bring the contents slowly to boiling-point. When quite boiling add a teacupful of cold water, and again bring to boiling-point. Now draw the pan aside, simmer gently for a few minutes, skimming meanwhile, and when quite clear use as required.

TOMATO JAM

To every lb. of ripe tomatoes allow 1 lb. of sugar. Scald the tomatoes and remove the skins. Cut open the fruit and remove the seeds. Put the fruit and sugar together in a pan, and add the juice of 2 lemons to every 3 lb. of fruit and sugar, and a small teaspoonful of ground ginger. Crush the fruit with a wooden spoon, and mix the whole well together. Boil slowly for about 2 hours, keeping it well stirred and skimmed.

Strawberries

TOMATOES (PRESERVE OF)

Take 7 lb. of firm, ripe tomatoes, 3 ½ lb. of sugar, 1 oz. each of cloves, allspice and cinnamon and 1 pint of vinegar.

Scald, drain and peel the tomatoes. Tie the spices in muslin, boil them for about 5 minutes with the sugar in the vinegar, then add the tomatoes, and simmer very gently for about ½ an hour. Keep closely covered in a dry, cool place.

VEGETABLE MARROW JAM

Take some nice young marrows, peel them, remove the seeds, cut them into thin slices and then into fine shreds. Make a syrup with 1 lb. of Demerara sugar to 1 pint of water, when it is boiling pour it over the marrows, and allow them to soak for 2 days and 2 nights in a covered jar or a basin, then strain off the syrup, and allow 1 lb. of loaf sugar to 1 lb. of marrow, also the rind and juice of 1 lemon, and 1 oz. of whole ginger tied up in muslin. Place in a saucepan, boil slowly till clear, then add a small glass of whisky or brandy (optional). Pour into jars, tie down, and set in a cool place.

Note: Allow 2 quarts of syrup to 6 lb. of fruit.

Marrow

VEGETABLE MARROW PRESERVE

Take 3 or 4 young vegetable marrows weighing about 6 lb. Peel them rather thinly, cut in half, and remove the seeds, then cut each half into thick slices and subsequently into dice or cubes. Put the vegetable marrow, and its weight in loaf sugar, into a preserving-pan with a quart [2 pints] of water. Boil gently for about 20 minutes; pour into a bowl and return all the liquid to the pan. Add 2 oz. of root or stem ginger previously bruised and tied in a piece of muslin, add also the thinly-cut rind and strained juice of 4 lemons. Boil for about ½ an hour; then add the marrow and boil up, skim and cook gently for another ½ an hour. Remove the ginger, fill the preserve into jars, and cover in the usual manner.

WATER-MELON, PRESERVED

Have ready 1 water-melon, 1 lb. of loaf sugar, ½ a pint of water, a little lemon-juice, ground ginger and vine leaves.

Pare and halve the melon, remove the soft part, and cut the outer part into small but rather thick slices. Place them in a preserving-pan between layers of vine leaves, barely cover with cold water, and cook, keeping the preparation just below simmering-point until half cooked. Drain, cover with cold water, and let it remain thus for about 3 hours, changing the water twice. Boil the sugar and ½ a pint of water to a syrup (more may be required for a large melon, but the quantity should be increased without altering the proportions), place the slices of melon carefully in it, and simmer gently for about 15 minutes. Drain the melon from the syrup, spread it on a dish in the sun for 3 hours, then repeat the process. The process is repeated for the third time after another interval of 3 hours, but before putting the melon into the syrup for the last time it should be flavoured to taste with ground ginger and lemon-juice, and boiled for a few minutes. Lift the slices of melon carefully into pots, pour the syrup over, cover closely, and store in a dry, cool place.

Making Blackberry Jam by Vladimir Makovsky (1876)

CHAPTER III

RECIPES FOR MARMALADE

APPLE MARMALADE

Peel, core and quarter 2 lb. of apples, place them in a jar with 4 oz. of sugar and 1 oz. of butter, and stand the jar in a saucepan containing boiling water, or, when more convenient, in a cool oven. Cook until soft, pass through a fine sieve, and use for filling turnovers, or other kinds of pastry.

APRICOT MARMALADE (*See* Apricot Jam)

CITRON MARMALADE (*See* Lemon Marmalade)

GRAPE MARMALADE

Remove the grape stalks, put the fruit into a preserving-pan, barely cover with boiling water, and simmer gently until perfectly soft, but the grapes must not be allowed to break. Drain well, pass through a fine sieve, and return the pulp to the pan. To each pint add from 12 to 16 oz. of preserving sugar, according to degree of sweetness required, and boil from 20 to 25 minutes, reckoning from the time the entire mass reaches boiling-point. Turn into jars, cover with paper brushed over on both sides with white of egg, and store in a cool, dry place.

GRATED MARMALADE

Take 12 large Seville oranges, 2 lemons and some preserving sugar.

Grate the rinds of 6 oranges, remove all the white pith, and throw it away. Remove and throw away both rind and pith of the remaining 6 oranges. Weigh the oranges, and to each lb. allow 1 lb. of sugar. Divide into sections, scrape out the pulp, and soak the pips and pith in a little cold water. Place the sugar, juice of the 2 lemons, orange-rind, pulp and juice in a preserving-pan, add the water strained from the pips and pith, and boil gently until the marmalade jellies quickly when tested on a cold plate. Cover the jars closely, and store them in a dry, cool place.

GREENGAGE MARMALADE (See Greengage Jam)

LEMON MARMALADE

Place the lemons in a preserving-pan, cover them with cold water, and boil them gently for about 2 hours, during which time the water must be drained off and replaced by fresh boiling water at least three times. Let them cool slightly, slice thinly, remove all the pips, and weigh the fruit. To each lb. allow 2 lb. of loaf sugar and 1 pint of the water the lemons were last boiled in, and boil these together until a thin syrup is obtained. Then add the prepared fruit, and boil until the marmalade jellies when tested on a cold plate. Cover closely with paper brushed over with white of egg, and store in a cool, dry place.

LEMON MARMALADE II

Prepare the lemons as directed in the preceding recipe, then weigh them. Take an equal weight of sour cooking apples, pare, core, slice them, and stew them gently until reduced to a pulp. Add the weight of the apple pulp to that of the sliced lemons; to each lb. allow 2 lb. of preserving sugar, and 1 pint of the water the lemons were last boiled in. Boil the sugar and water to a thin-syrup, add the fruit, and boil gently until the marmalade sets quickly when tested on a cold plate. Pour into pots, cover with paper brushed over on both sides with white of egg, and store in a cool, dry place.

LEMON MARMALADE III

Take 6 lemons or more to make up the weight of 2 lb. and 4 lb. loaf sugar.

Choose the lemons so that they are clear and smooth. Put them in a copper stewpan, and cover well with water, boil them for about 2 hours, changing the water two or three times during the process. Drain them, keep the water the lemons were last boiled in. Cut the lemons in halves longways, and slice them as finely as possible, removing all the pips. Take 3 pints of the lemon water and put it with the sugar in a copper sugar-boiler on to boil. Remove the scum, and let boil for about 15 minutes. Add the fruit and boil again until it becomes clear. Strain off the fruit when cold, boil up the syrup again, add the fruit, give it another boil, then put into jars, let it cool and cover, and store in the usual manner.

ORANGE MARMALADE

Take 12 Seville oranges, 2 lemons and some preserving sugar.

Slice the fruit thinly, removing inner pith and pips. Weigh it, and to each lb. add 3 pints of cold water. Let the whole remain covered in an earthenware vessel for 3 days, then turn

Lemons

the preparation into a preserving-pan and boil gently until quite tender. Let it cool, weigh again, and to each lb. of fruit add 1 lb. of sugar. Bring to boiling-point, skim well, and cook gently until the syrup stiffens quickly when tested on a cold plate. Turn into pots, cover with paper brushed over on both sides with white of egg, and store in a cool, dry place.

ORANGE MARMALADE II

Have ready 24 Seville oranges, their weight in preserving sugar, and 2 pints of cold water.

Take off the rinds of the oranges, divide the pulp into small pieces, and remove the pips. Boil the rinds in water for 2 hours, changing it two or three times to reduce the bitter flavour; when quite tender, drain well, and shred them finely. Boil the sugar and water to a syrup, skimming well meanwhile, then add the pulp and shredded rinds. Boil gently for about ½ an hour, or until the marmalade sets quickly when tested on a cold plate, then pour into pots and cover down with paper brushed over on both sides with white of egg. Keep the marmalade in a cool, dry place until required for use.

ORANGE MARMALADE (Transparent)

Take 4 lb. of Seville oranges, 8 lb. of preserving sugar, 6 pints of water and 2 or 3 whites of eggs.

Remove the rinds of the oranges, and scrape away the white pith. Shred the rind finely, cover with water, boil gently until tender, then strain and preserve the liquid. Strip every particle of pith from the oranges, slice them, and remove the pips, and soak these in a little cold water. Simmer the remainder of the water and the sliced oranges for about 2 hours, then drain through a fine hair sieve or cloth, but do not squeeze the pulp. Replace the liquid in the pan, add the liquid in which the rind was cooked and the strained water from the pips, bring nearly to boiling-point, and clarify with white of eggs. Strain until clear, replace in the pan, add the sugar, boil gently until the syrup jellies when tested on a cold plate, and add the orange-rind. Simmer gently for some 10 minutes longer, then turn into pots, cover closely, and store in a dry, cool place.

ORANGE MARMALADE MADE WITH HONEY

Boil the rinds of some oranges until tender, then shred them finely. Remove the pith and pips, measure the pulp, and to each pint allow 1lb. of honey and ½ a lb. of the prepared rinds. Simmer gently for about 40 minutes, stirring frequently, then turn the marmalade into jars or glasses, and cover these with parchment. Store the jars away in a cool, dry place.

PEACH MARMALADE (See Peach and Pineapple Marmalade)

Recipes for Marmalade

Peach

PEACH AND PINEAPPLE MARMALADE

Procure 7 lb. of peaches, 1 large ripe pineapple, 3 lemons and 6 lb. of sugar.

Pare and slice the pineapple, peel and stone the peaches, crack ½ the stones and remove the kernels. Put the peaches and pineapple into a preserving-pan with just a little water to protect the bottom layer, heat slowly to simmering-point, and afterwards cook gently for about ½ an hour. Add the sugar gradually, so as not to reduce the temperature below simmering-point, the strained juice of the lemons and the kernels, and boil gently for about 20 minutes, skimming when necessary. Pour into earthenware or glass jars, cover closely, and store in a cool, dry place.

PINEAPPLE MARMALADE

Peel, core and slice the pineapples, and either pound or grate them finely, preferably the latter. To each lb. of pulp add 14 oz. of loaf sugar. Boil the pulp and sugar together until thick and clear, then turn into pots, cover first with brandied paper, and then with parchment. Store in a cool, dry place.

QUINCE MARMALADE

Pare the fruit, put it into a preserving-pan with as much water as will just cover the bottom of the pan, and stew gently until reduced to a pulp. Pass through a hair sieve, weigh the pulp, replace it in the pan, add to each lb. of pulp ¾ of a lb. of preserving sugar, and cook very gently until the marmalade sets quickly when tested on a cold plate. Turn into pots, cover with paper brushed over with white of egg, and store in a cool, dry place.

RHUBARB MARMALADE

Wipe, string, and cut the rhubarb into short lengths. To each lb. allow 2 tablespoonfuls of sugar and ¼ of a teaspoonful of ground ginger. Put the rhubarb, sugar and ginger in a jar, place the jar in a rather cool oven, or in a saucepan containing boiling water, and cook until soft. Pass through a fine sieve, and use for filling turnovers and similar kinds of pastry.

TANGERINE MARMALADE

Have ready 30 tangerines, double their weight in loaf or preserving sugar, 6 lemons and enough cold water to float the tangerines.

Wash the tangerines in water and wipe them. Place them in a preserving-pan with enough cold water to float them, and let them boil till the rinds are soft. Drain off the water. Cut each tangerine in quarters, remove the pips, place in a basin containing a pint of cold water, and let them soak for 12 hours. Remove all the pulp from the rind, and mash it well, slice the peel as thinly as possible. Put the sugar in a preserving-pan with the water from the pips, and the strained juice of the lemons. Reduce this to the consistency of thick syrup, then add the tangerine pulp and rinds, and boil for about ½ an hour. Fill into dry jars, and when cold cover them with parchment.

Note: Before removing the marmalade from the fire, pour a little on a plate which should set like jelly when cold, if not, reduce it a little longer.

TOMATO MARMALADE

Procure 7 lb. of ripe tomatoes, 8 lb. of loaf sugar, ½ a pint of water and 6 lemons.

Remove the stalks from the tomatoes, wipe them with a cloth, blanch, skin, and cut each into halves; peel the lemons, cut them into slices, and remove the pips. Put the sugar and water into a copper sugar-pan, stir gently over the fire until the sugar is dissolved, skim, and boil to a syrup; put in the tomatoes and lemons and boil quickly, stirring from time to time. Remove the scum which rises to the top. When the marmalade is sufficiently cooked it should hang on the spatula or spoon in thick gelatinous flakes. When done, fill into glass jars or earthenware pots, cover with parchment paper, and store away.

Tangerines

Picking Rhubarb by Nikolai Astrup (1911)

Recipes for Marmalade

Bodegón de naranjas [Still Life with Oranges] by Rafael Romero Barros (1863)

CHAPTER IV

RECIPES FOR FRUIT JELLIES

The preserving pan and spoon

These pans are best made of copper or brass, as the preserve does not then so readily boil over or stick to the pan and burn. Enamelled ones, however, are cheaper and quite satisfactory if properly used. The spoon should be a wooden one.

The Preserving Pan and Spoon

Straining for jelly

When the fruit is quite soft and the juice has been extracted, the juice should be strained through a fine sieve or jelly-bag. Press the fruit to extract all the juice, but do not rub the pulp through the sieve.

Straining for Jelly

FRUIT jellies are prepared with juices from fruits containing pectin or vegetable jelly with the addition of an equal quantity of sugar.

The best fruits, and those most adapted for making jellies, are red currants, gooseberries, apples, quinces, Seville oranges, etc.

Care should be taken not to boil jellies too much; for if they are over-boiled their colour is spoiled, and they become ropy, like treacle.

APPLE JELLY

All sour or tart apples make excellent jelly. Wash the apples and remove all unsound parts. Cut them into pieces without paring or removing the core. Place in an earthenware preserving-pan, add enough water to cover, and cook till tender. Drain the juice, and allow ¾ of a lb. of loaf sugar to each pint. Measure 3 pints of juice into the preserving-pan, boil about 15 minutes, then add the sugar and cook till it forms a jelly when cold.

APPLE JELLY II

Take 10 lb. of apples and 10 pints of water.

Rub the apples well with a dry cloth, but do not pare them. Cut them into quarters, remove the cores, and put them into a preserving-pan with the water. Simmer until perfectly soft, but not broken, then strain off the liquid without squeezing the pulp. If not clear, pass through a jelly-bag or clean dry cloth, until it becomes so. To each pint of liquid obtained allow 1 lb. of sugar and the juice of 2 lemons, and simmer gently until a little, poured on a cold plate, almost immediately begins to stiffen. Pour into pots, cover closely, and store in a cool, dry place.

Note: The apple pulp should be sweetened, flavoured with ginger or cinnamon, and made into jam.

APPLE JELLY (Another Way)

To 6 lb. of apples allow 3 pints of water; to every quart of juice allow 2 lb. of loaf sugar and the juice of ½ a lemon.

Pare, core and cut the apples into slices, and put them into a jar, with water in the above proportion. Place them in a cool oven, with the jar well covered, and when the juice is thoroughly drawn and the apples are quite soft, strain them through a jelly-bag. To each quart of juice allow 2 lb. of loaf sugar, which should be crushed to small lumps and put in the preserving-pan with the juice. Boil these together for rather more than ½ an hour, remove the scum as it rises, add the lemon-juice just before it is done, and put the jelly into pots.

Apple

APRICOT JELLY

To each lb. of ripe apricots, weighed after the stones and skins are removed, allow 1 lb. of preserving sugar and the juice of 1 lemon.

Remove the skins, break the apricots in halves, and blanch the kernels. Weigh the fruit, put it into a preserving-pan with an equal amount of sugar, and add the prepared kernels and lemon-juice. Simmer gently, stir frequently until reduced to the consistency of thick marmalade, then pour into small pots. Cover first with paper moistened with salad oil, and afterwards with tissue paper brushed over with white of egg; store in a dry, cool place.

BARBERRY JELLY

Wash the ripe barberries in cold water, and put them into a jar with a close-fitting lid, place the jar on the stove or in a moderate oven, in a tin half full of boiling water, and simmer gently for about 2 hours. Strain the juice into a preserving pan, to each pint add 1 lb. of loaf sugar, and bring to boiling point. Boil for about 10 minutes, removing the scum as it rises, then pour into small pots. Cover with paper brushed over with white of egg.

BLACKBERRY JELLY

Take 6lb. of blackberries, 6 medium-sized sour apples, the juice of 1 lemon and ¾ of a pint of water.

Stalk the blackberries, wipe, peel, core and slice the apples. Place the apples, water and lemon-juice into a preserving-pan. Cook until the apples are soft, then add the blackberries and continue to boil until they are soft. Strain off the liquid through a fine hair sieve or cloth. Do not rub the fruit, only press it lightly to extract the juice.

Wash out the pan, allow 1 lb. of sugar to each pint of juice and boil in the pan until it will jelly if a little is cooled on a plate. Pour it into dry, warm jars, cover, tie down, and store in a cool place.

Blackberries

BLACK-CURRANT JELLY

Remove the stalks from the black currants and put the fruit into a jar placed in a saucepan of boiling water, and simmer until their juice is extracted. Strain the juice into a preserving-pan, to each pint add ¾ of a lb. of preserving sugar, and boil gently until the jelly stiffens when a little is tested on a cold plate. Pour into small pots, cover with paper brushed over with white of egg, fasten securely so as to exclude the air, and store in a cool, dry place until required for use.

Crab apple

CRAB-APPLE JELLY

Take 4 lb. of crab-apples (Siberian), 4 pints of water, 6 cloves, 1 inch of ginger and 1 lb. of sugar to each pint of strained liquid.

Halve the crab-apples with a silver knife. Place them in the water, add the cloves and ginger, simmer until tender, then drain well, but do not squeeze the apples. Replace the drained liquid in the pan, add the sugar, boil until the syrup jellies quickly when tested on a cold plate, then pour into small jars or glasses. Cover securely with parchment, and store in a cool, dry place.

CRANBERRY JELLY

Procure ½ lb. of cranberries, 6 oz. of sugar, a pinch of soda, a teaspoonful of lemon-juice, 1½ gills of water.

Pick over and wash the cranberries, put them in a stew-pan with the water and soda. Remove the scum as soon as it begins to boil, then add the sugar, and boil gently for about 20 minutes, and keep covered whilst boiling. Remove the lid and add the lemon-juice, reduce briskly for a few minutes until the liquid stiffens; strain into a wetted mould or any earthen vessel, allow it to set in a cool place, and turn out when required. This is not exactly a sauce, although the Americans usually describe it as such. It forms a very excellent and most appropriate accompaniment with roast turkey.

CHERRY JELLY

Prepare as for Red-Currant Jelly, measuring the fruit in the proportion of 3 lb. of cherries to 1 lb. of red currants.

DAMSON JELLY

The damsons must be firm, dry and ripe. Remove the stalks, put the fruit into a large jar or stew-pot, cover closely, place it in a boiling-pot of cold water, and cook very slowly until the plums are perfectly tender. Strain the juice through a jelly-bag, or fine cloth, into a preserving-pan, add from 8 to 10 oz. of preserving sugar to each pint of juice, and boil until the jelly sets quickly when tested on a cold plate. Pour into pots, cover closely with paper brushed over with white of egg, and fasten so as to exclude the air. Store in a cool, dry place.

Note: The fruit from which the juice has been extracted may be converted into Damson Cheese.

GOOSEBERRY JELLY

To each pint of gooseberries allow ½ a pint of water; to each pint of juice obtained from these add 1 lb. of sugar.

Put the fruit and water into a preserving-pan, and boil slowly until reduced to a pulp. Strain through a jelly-bag of fine cloth until clear, then put it into the preserving-pan with the sugar, and boil until it will set when a little is poured on a cold plate. Turn into small pots, cover with paper brushed over with white of egg, fasten securely down so as to exclude the air completely, and store the jelly in a cool, dry place.

GRAPE JELLY

To each lb. of fruit add ¼ of a pint of cold water. To each pint of juice obtained from these add 1 lb. of either loaf or preserving sugar.

Remove the stalks, put the fruit and the water into a preserving-pan, and simmer very gently until the grapes are soft. Strain the juice through a jelly-bag or fine cloth until clear, replace it in the pan, and boil rapidly for about ½ an hour. Add the sugar and continue the boiling until the jelly sets quickly when tested on a cold plate. As the scum rises it should be carefully removed. When ready pour the jelly into small pots, cover closely, and store in a cool, dry place.

MEDLAR JELLY

Put ripe medlars into a preserving-pan after cutting off the tops. Cover with cold water, boil slowly for some hours, then strain off the juice through a fine hair sieve. Allow about 1 lb. of preserving sugar to each pint of juice. Boil the juice and sugar together over a quick fire, stirring all the time, from 20 to 30 minutes, or until the mixture thickens and is sufficiently set if dropped and cooled on a plate. As soon as the mixture is sufficiently cooled pour it into clean dry jars, tie down and store in a cool place.

Medlars

LOQUAT JELLY

May be made as directed for Quince Jelly, but a little less sugar should be used.

ORANGE JELLY (Seville)

Procure some fine Seville oranges, squeeze out the juice, filter it through a flannel bag, and proceed and finish as for Red-Currant Jelly.

recipes for Fruit Jellies

POMEGRANATE JELLY

Mash the seeds of 6 very ripe pomegranates, mix with the juice of 2 oranges and 2 lemons, adding the rind of one. Strain through a cloth or jelly-bag, and finish as for Barberry Jelly. Pour into the mould a layer of jelly. When it is set, place on it a layer of pomegranate, and then another layer of jelly, and so on until the mould is filled.

PRICKLY PEAR OR CACTUS FRUIT JELLY

Have at hand 3 lb. of prickly pears or cactus fruit, 3 pints of water, lemons and preserving sugar.

Rub off the spines very carefully with a thick cloth. Cut the fruit in half and add the water. Boil till the fruit is almost in a pulp. Strain away the liquid, and for every pint allow the juice of a lemon and a lb. of sugar. Simmer gently, removing any scum until the syrup jellies. Cover down with parchment paper and store for future use.

QUINCE JELLY

Select the fruit ripe and of fine flavour. The orange quince is considered the best. Wash well and rub the fruit with a cloth. The best part of the quince can be used for bottling and preserving. Make the jelly from the rind and hard knotty parts, with the addition of some of the whole fruit. Remove the seeds or core portion. Cover the fruit with water, stew gently until tender, and then drain; ¾ of a lb. of cane sugar to each pint of juice is sufficient. Measure 3 pints of juice into the preserving-pan, boil for about 15 minutes, add sugar and proceed as previously directed.

QUINCE JELLY II

Take 4 lb. of fine quinces - not too ripe - slice them into a pan with enough water to cover. Put the pan on the fire, and boil them until tender. Pour the mixture through a flannel bag, and for each pint of filtered juice add ¾ of a lb. of sugar. Boil it on a clear fire for 10 to 20 minutes, remove the scum, and finish as for Red-Currant Jelly.

QUINCE JELLY III

Pare and slice the quinces, and put them into a preserving-pan with sufficient water to float them. Boil them until the fruit is reduced to a pulp. Strain off the clear juice, and to each pint allow 1 lb. of loaf sugar. Boil the juice and sugar together for about ¾ of an hour, remove all the scum as it rises, and when the jelly appears firm upon a little being poured on a plate, pour into small pots. The residue left on the sieve will answer to make

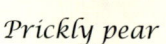

Prickly pear

a common marmalade for immediate use, by boiling it with ½ a lb. of common sugar to every lb. of pulp.

RASPBERRY JELLY

Let the raspberries be freshly gathered, quite ripe, and picked from the stalks; put them into a large jar after breaking the fruit a little with a wooden spoon, and place the jar, covered, in a saucepan of boiling water. When the juice is well drawn, which will be from ¾ to 1 hour, strain the fruit through a fine hair sieve or cloth, measure the juice, and to each pint allow ¼ of a lb. of loaf sugar. Put the juice and sugar into a preserving-pan, place it over the fire, and boil gently until the jelly thickens upon a little being poured on a cold plate; carefully remove all the scum as it rises, pour the jelly into small pots, cover down, and keep in a dry place. This jelly answers for making raspberry cream, and for flavouring various sweet dishes.

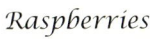

Raspberries

RED-CURRANT JELLY

Strip the currants from the stalks, place the fruit in a saucepan with a little water and simmer for about ½ an hour until all the juice is extracted. Then strain through a jelly-bag or fine cloth into a preserving-pan. To each pint add 1 lb. of loaf or preserving sugar, and boil slowly for about ¾ of an hour, skim well. When the jelly is sufficiently boiled, it will set quickly if a little is put on a cold plate. Pour into small dry pots, tie them down in the usual way.

RED-CURRANT JELLY II

Take 3 lb. of red currants and 1 lb. of white currants. Pick and wash them and mash them through a coarse sieve, then put them into a pan with a very little water. Put the pan on the fire, and stir the fruit until it boils. Withdraw from the fire, remove the scum, and pass the juice through a flannel bag. Measure and boil this for 10 to 15 minutes on a clear fire, add the cane sugar in equal quantities. Boil again, remove the scum, and put the jelly into clean, dry jars. When cold it should be covered with pieces of paper dipped in brandy, and the whole covered by parchment. Store in a cool, dry place.

TIPPAREE JELLY

Have ready some Tipparee pods (Cape gooseberries), sugar and lemon-juice. Wipe the pods, cover them with cold water, simmer gently until soft, then drain through a jelly-bag, but do not squeeze the pulp. Measure the liquor carefully, and to each pint add 1 lb. of sugar and 1 dessertspoonful of lemon-juice, and simmer gently for about ½ an hour, skimming meanwhile. Pour the jelly into jars, cover and tie down in the usual way. The jars should be stored in a cool, dry place.

WHITE-CURRANT JELLY

Pick the currants from the stalk, and put them into a jar. Place the jar in a saucepan of boiling water, simmer gently until the juice is extracted, then strain through a jelly-bag or fine cloth into a preserving-pan. To each pint allow from ¾ to 1 lb. of preserving sugar, according to taste, and boil gently until the jelly quickly sets, when a little is poured on a cold plate. Turn into small pots, cover with tissue paper brushed over with white of egg, fasten securely, and keep the jelly in a cool, dry place.

CHAPTER V

PRESERVED AND CRYSTALLIZED FRUITS

Making the syrup
The syrup is boiled to the "large blow" degree (233° F.); it is then cooled a little before the dried fruit is dipped into it.

Making the Syrup

Dipping the fruit
The fruit must be thoroughly coated with syrup; it is then rolled in crushed loaf sugar and afterwards dried.

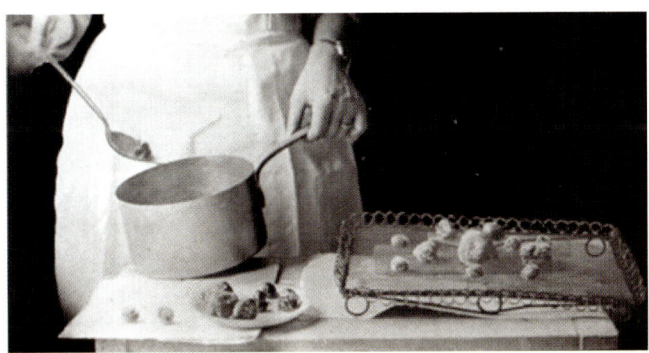

Dipping the Fruit

THE PREPARATION of Preserved Fruits requires great care and attention.

There are two kinds of preserves – "wet" and "dry". The former are kept in their syrup, and the latter are crystallized, or frosted with sugar.

In order to obtain satisfactory results, the fruits should be specially selected for preserving purposes, and should be gathered early, just before they are quite ripe.

All fruit should be carefully blanched, in a sufficient quantity of boiling water, and in a suitable pan with a flat bottom. The water should only be allowed to simmer.

DRY PRESERVES

Any of the fruits that have been preserved in syrup may be converted into dry preserves, by first draining them from the syrup and then drying them on a stove or in a very moderate oven, adding to them a quantity of powdered loaf sugar, which will gradually penetrate the fruit, while the fluid parts of the syrup gently evaporate. They should be dried on the stove or in the oven on a sieve, and turned every 6 or 8 hours, fresh powdered sugar being sifted over them each time they are turned. Currants and cherries may be preserved whole in this manner in bunches. Orange and lemon chips are thus preserved. After being thoroughly dried they should be stored in air-tight tins in a cool, dry place.

GLACÉ AND CRYSTALLIZED FRUITS

Before fruit can be subjected to the final process by which it is preserved for use in these two forms, it must first be boiled in syrup. The fruit to be candied or iced is dried before the fire or in a cool oven, the syrup in which it was cooked being meanwhile boiled to the "large blow" degree (233° F.). When the syrup has cooled a little, the fruit should be dipped into it until thoroughly coated, and then dried, when they will have a transparent coating. Fruit to be crystallized should, immediately on its removal from the syrup, be rolled in crushed loaf sugar and afterwards dried.

APPLES, TO PRESERVE IN QUARTERS

Take 8 lb. of apples, 6 lb. of sugar, 6 pints of water and the juice of 4 lemons.

Peel, quarter and core the apples. Place the apple peeling and cores in the water, add the sugar, simmer gently for about 25 minutes, and strain until clear. Replace the syrup in the pan, add the apples and lemon-juice, and simmer gently until the apples are tender, but not broken. Place them in jars or wide-necked bottles, pour the syrup over them, and cover the preparation so as completely to exclude the air. Store in a cool, dry place.

APRICOTS, TO DRY (*See* Greengages, to Preserve Dry)

APRICOTS, CRYSTALLIZED

Proceed as in preparing Crystallized Greengages.

APRICOTS, PRESERVED

Choose some fine, yellow apricots - not too ripe - run the point of a small knife into the fruit near the stalk, and work it slightly round the stone, which can then be gently squeezed out. Blanch the apricots in boiling water until tender when they will rise to the surface, then drop them into cold water. Prepare a syrup and boil it to the "hard blow". Put in the apricots and boil up twice, then withdraw from the fire, remove the scum, and finish as with Greengages.

A Jar of Apricots

BARBERRIES IN BUNCHES

Prepare some small pieces of clean white wood 3 inches long and ¼ of an inch wide; tie the fruit to these in nice bunches. Have ready some clear syrup; put in the barberries, and simmer them in it for about ½ an hour on two successive days, and covering them each time with the syrup when cold. When the fruit looks perfectly clear it is sufficiently done, and should be stored away in pots, with the syrup poured over. Or, if preferred, the berries may be candied (see Cherries, Dried and Greengages, to Preserve Dry).

BEETROOT, PRESERVED

Peel the beetroots, put them into a preserving-pan with water barely to cover them, and boil them gently for about 20 minutes. To each lb. of beetroot allow ½ a lb. of preserving sugar, the juice of ½ a lemon, and the finely-grated rind of ¼ of a lemon. Add vanilla pod and stick cinnamon to taste, and continue the cooking until the beetroots are quite tender, then drain them from the syrup, cut them into convenient lengths, and place them in jars of suitable size. Boil the syrup rapidly until it is quite thick, skimming when necessary meanwhile, and pour it into the jars. Cover closely so as completely to exclude the air, and keep in a cool, dry place.

CHERRIES, DRIED

Cherries may be put into a slow oven and thoroughly dried before they begin to change colour. They should then be taken out of the oven, tied in bunches, and stored away in a dry place. In the winter they may be cooked with sugar for dessert, the same as Normandy pippins. Particular care must be taken that the oven be not too hot. Another method of drying cherries is to stone them and put them into a preserving-pan with plenty of loaf sugar strewed among them. They should be simmered till the fruit shrivels, then they should be strained from the juice. The cherries should then be placed in an oven cool enough to dry without baking them. About 6 oz. of sugar will be required for 1 lb. of cherries, and the same syrup may be used again to do another quantity of fruit.

CHERRIES, RED, PRESERVED OR CRYSTALLIZED

Procure some fine Kentish cherries, stone them, and put them into a pan with sufficient boiling syrup to cover them. Boil up three or four times, withdraw from the fire, remove the scum, and finish as for Greengages.

CHERRIES, TO PRESERVE

Procure some sound, ripe cooking cherries. To each lb. allow ½ a lb. of preserving sugar and ¼ of a pint of water.

Remove the stones carefully, keeping the fruit as whole as possible. Boil the sugar and water to a syrup, add the cherries, simmer them gently for about 15 minutes, then turn both fruit and syrup into a large basin, and put aside until the following day. Strain the syrup into a preserving-pan; to each pint add from 4 to 6 oz. of sugar, according to taste, bring to boiling-point, skim well, then put in the fruit and simmer gently for about 10 minutes. Pour into jars, cover with paper dipped in brandy, stretch tissue paper brushed over with white of egg on top, and fasten down securely. Store in a cool, dry place.

Note: The flavour may be considerably improved by substituting the juice of either red or white currants for the water.

CHERRIES, WHITE, PRESERVED OR CRYSTALLIZED

Proceed as for Red Cherries, taking care to select thoroughly sound fruit.

CHESTNUTS, CRYSTALLIZED

Choose some fine chestnuts. Take off the outside skin, and blanch them in sufficient boiling water until a needle runs through them easily. Then take off the inner or thin yellow skin, and drop them into warm water. Drain and put them into syrup, and let them simmer gently until the syrup becomes thick - the syrup should never be allowed to boil. Take out the chestnuts, and drain them on a sieve. Boil some syrup to the "small blow" (230°) in a small pan, and just before it is quite cold work it against the side edges of the pan. Into this dip the chestnuts with a fork, place on trays, and dry them in a cool oven.

Cherries

CURRANTS, SPICED (*See* Plums, Spiced)

DAMSONS, BAKED, FOR KEEPING

Fruit for preserving in this manner should be perfectly sound, and not over-ripe. Remove the stalks, but not the stones. To each lb. of fruit allow ½ a lb. of sugar. Place the fruit and sugar in a large stew-jar in alternate layers, cover closely, and bake in a very cool oven until the plums are tender. Pack the plums closely in large jars, pour the syrup over, and when quite cold cover with white paper cut to the size of the jar. Have ready some mutton suet melted but on the point of setting, pour it into the jars to the depth of about ½ an inch, stretch pieces of bladder or paper brushed over with white of egg over the jars, and fasten them securely. If stored in a cool, dry place, the fruit will keep good for 3 or 4 months.

FIGS, TO PRESERVE

Procure some green figs. To each lb. allow 1 lb. of sugar and ½ a pint of water.

Make a slit across the top of each fig, cover them with brine that will float an egg, and let them remain for 8 days. Drain well, boil gently in a little water until quite tender, then drain again and cover with cold water. Change the water daily for 3 days, and on the third day have ready a syrup made of the sugar and water in the proportions given above. Boil the figs in the syrup for about 10 minutes, repeat the process daily for 3 or 4 days, until the figs are tender and green. Place them in jars or bottles, add the syrup, cover closely, and store in a dry, cool place.

FIGS, PRESERVED

Choose some figs just before they are quite ripe, prick them all over, and drop them into cold water. Blanch them until tender, then drop them into cold water again, and finish as for Apricots.

Figs

FROSTED FRUIT

FRUIT of nearly every description may be frosted or iced by dipping it in beaten white of egg, and afterwards in crushed loaf sugar, the process being repeated until a sufficiently thick coating is obtained. Pineapples should be sliced; pears, peaches and plums should be halved after removing the skins; cherries, strawberries and similar fruit are iced with the stems on; and from oranges and lemons every particle of pith is removed before dividing the former into sections and the latter into slices.

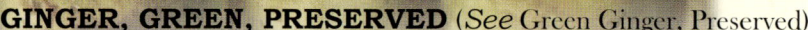

Greengages

GINGER, GREEN, PRESERVED (*See* Green Ginger, Preserved)

GOOSEBERRIES, GREEN, PRESERVED

Choose some fine large gooseberries - not too ripe - pick them and blanch them, add a little soda or salt to keep them green, and finish as for Greengages.

GREENGAGES, CRYSTALLIZED

Take the greengages out of the syrup, drain them on a sieve, place them on wire trays, and put them in the oven until dry, or crystallized. Then place them in suitable boxes.

GREENGAGES, PRESERVED

Choose some good greengages, take a bodkin and prick them all over, then drop them into a pan of cold water. Place the pan on the fire, blanch the fruit, and remove the pan when just at boiling-point. Take out the greengages with a skimmer when they float on the surface of the water, and drop them into cold water. Drain them on a sieve. Then prepare a plain syrup, boil it to the "Small Thread" (215° F.), add the greengages, and let them gently boil. Withdraw from the fire and remove the scum, pour them into an earthen pan, and next day drain the syrup off. Add more sugar, and boil up again to the "Large Thread" (217° F.). Repeat this process for 6 days, the last time boiling the sugar to the "Large Pearl" (222° F.).

Note: Soft fruits should not be boiled in the syrup, but require the boiling syrup to be poured on them. Preserved fruits should be kept in a dry place - not too warm, as heat causes fermentation, and damp makes them mouldy.

GREENGAGES PRESERVED IN SYRUP

To each lb. of fruit allow 1 lb. of either loaf or preserving sugar, and ¼ of a pint of water.

Proceed exactly as in the recipe for Greengage Jam, with the exception of removing the stones before putting the fruit into the syrup. Boil the fruit for about 10 minutes on 3 consecutive days, adding on the last day half the kernels, which should be previously blanched. Throughout the whole process the scum must be carefully removed as it rises, otherwise the syrup will not be clear.

GREENGAGES, TO PRESERVE DRY

To each lb. of fruit allow 1 lb. of sugar and ¼ of a pint of water.

For this purpose the fruit must be used before it is quite ripe, and part of the stalk must be left on. Weigh the fruit, rejecting all that is in the least degree blemished, and put it into a lined saucepan with the sugar and water, which should have been previously boiled together to a syrup. Boil the fruit in this for about 10 minutes, remove it from the fire, and drain the greengages. The next day boil up the syrup, put in the fruit again, let it simmer for a few minutes, then drain the syrup away. Continue this process for 5 or 6 days, and the last time place the greengages, when drained, on a hair sieve, and put them in an oven to dry. Keep them in a box, with paper between each layer, in a place free from damp.

GREEN GINGER, TO PRESERVE

Put the ginger regularly every night and morning for a fortnight into fresh boiling water. Remove the outside skin with a sharp knife, boil it in water until it is quite soft, and slice it in thin slices. Make ready a syrup of 1 lb. of loaf sugar to ½ a pint of water, clarify it, and put the ginger into it. Boil until it is clear.

LEMONS, FANCY

Proceed in the same way as directed for Fancy Oranges.

LEMONS, TO PRESERVE WHOLE (*See* Oranges and Lemons, to Preserve Whole)

MANGOES, TO PRESERVE

Let the mangoes lie for a few hours in cold water, then peel them thinly and remove the stones. Cover with weak lime-water, and at the end of 1 hour drain well and place them in a preserving-pan. Barely cover with cold water, boil gently for about 10 minutes, and drain well. Replace the mangoes in the pan, cover with sugar syrup, boil gently until the sugar begins to crystallize, and, when cool, transfer carefully into jars or wide-necked bottles. During the first month the syrup must be examined from time to time, and if it appears at all thin it should be re-boiled. It may be necessary to repeat this process two or three times before finally corking down.

Mangoes

MELON, PRESERVED

Prepare the same as for Pineapple.

MULBERRIES, PRESERVED

Have ready some ripe mulberries and preserving sugar.

Put half the fruit into a jar, cover closely, place it on the stove in a large saucepan of cold water, and cook slowly until the juice is extracted. Strain, measure the juice, and put it into a preserving-pan or large stewpan with the addition of 2 lb. of sugar to each pint of juice. Bring to boiling-point, skim well, add the remainder of the fruit, and boil until it is half-cooked. Turn the whole into an earthenware vessel, unless the preserving-pan be lined with enamel, in which case they may remain in the pan. On the following day boil until the juice sets quickly when tested on a cold plate. Turn into pots, cover closely, and store in a cool, dry place.

NECTARINES, PRESERVED

Split the nectarines in halves, remove the stones, crack them and put the kernels aside. Weigh the fruit, put an equal amount of sugar into the preserving-pan, add ¼ of a pint of water to each lb. of sugar, and boil to a syrup. Now put in the fruit, boil very gently until it is quite tender, but not broken, then lift it out carefully with a spoon and put it into pots. Boil the syrup rapidly until it sets quickly when tested on a cold plate, pour it over the fruit, cover closely, and store in a cool, dry place.

ORANGES, FANCY

Choose some round, smooth oranges, cut on the rind any fancy designs, such as stars, circles, angles, etc. When the oranges are decorated, blanch them in boiling water until tender, and then drop them into cold water. Boil a plain syrup to the "Small Thread" (215° F.). Drain and dry the oranges, then drop them into the syrup. Boil up two or three times, removing the scum. Then finish as for other fruits.

ORANGES, GREEN, TO PRESERVE OR CRYSTALLIZE

Proceed exactly the same as in preparing greengages. The fruit must be very carefully selected.

ORANGES AND LEMONS, TO PRESERVE WHOLE

To 1 lb. of oranges allow 2 lb. of sugar and 1 pint of water; to lemons add 3 lb. of sugar and 1½ pints of water.

   At one end of each orange make a hole sufficiently large to admit a small spoon, and scoop out the pulp and juice. Cover the rinds with cold water, and let them remain for 3 days, changing the water two or three times daily. Drain, place them in the preserving-pan with sufficient cold water to cover them, simmer gently until tender, and drain well. Boil the sugar and water to a syrup, add the juice and pulp, boil gently for about 15 minutes, and pour the whole over the oranges. When quite cold, replace in the pan, simmer very gently for about ½ an hour, then turn into an earthenware vessel. On the following day boil up the syrup and pour it over the oranges; this process should be repeated on two or three consecutive days until the rinds are quite clear. Fill the oranges with syrup, place them in wide-necked jars, pour the remainder of the syrup over them, and cover closely. Store in a cool, dry place.

ORANGES, TO PRESERVE (*See* preceding recipe)

PEACHES, PRESERVED OR CRYSTALLIZED

Choose some fine yellow peaches, but not too ripe. Prick them all over with a large needle down to the stone, and proceed as with Apricots.

PEACHES, PRESERVED IN BRANDY

Peaches intended for preserving should be firm, sound, and not over-ripe. Take 6 lb. of peaches, 3 lb. of castor or powdered loaf sugar, and 3 pints of brandy.

Remove the stones, taking care to keep the fruit as whole as possible, place the fruit in a large jar, and cover each layer thickly with sugar. Add the brandy, cover closely, place the jar in a saucepan of boiling water, and cook gently until the brandy is on the point of boiling. Remove the fruit carefully to hot, dry, small pots, add to each an equal share of the hot brandy, and cover closely with paper brushed over with white of egg. Store in a cool, dry place.

Pear

PEARS, PRESERVED

Choose firm, sound, not over-ripe pears, and take an equal weight of loaf sugar.

Pare, halve, and core the pears. Put half the sugar into a preserving-pan, to each lb. add 2 pints of water, and boil to a thin syrup. Let it cool, put in the prepared fruit, and simmer very gently until half cooked. Turn the whole into an earthenware bowl, cover, and allow them to remain for 2 days. When ready, drain the syrup into a preserving-pan, add the remainder of the sugar and a tablespoonful of lemon-juice to each pint of liquid, and boil gently for about 15 minutes, skimming well meanwhile. Now put in the fruit, simmer very gently until quite tender, then transfer them carefully to jars, and pour over the syrup. Cover closely, and store in a cool, dry place.

PEARS, PRESERVED II

Take 8 lb. of firm, sound pears, 6 lb. of preserving sugar, the finely-grated rind and juice of 3 lemons and 2 inches of whole ginger.

Select a stew-jar with a close-fitting lid, cover the bottom to the depth of 1 inch with cold water, put in the fruit and sugar in layers, and add the ginger, lemon-rind and lemon juice.

Cover closely, place the jar in a saucepan of boiling water, and cook slowly until the pears are quite tender, but not broken. Put them carefully into jars, strain the syrup over them, and cover with papers brushed over on both sides with white of egg. The pears will keep good for 3 or 4 months if stored in a cool, dry place.

PEARS, RED, PRESERVED

Proceed as with White Pears. Add sufficient cochineal to give the pears a delicate, but not too deep a tint of red.

PEARS, WHITE, PRESERVED

Choose some fine large pears - not too ripe - prick them over, and blanch them until a pin's head runs easily through them. Drop them into cold water, pare off the rind very thinly, and prick them again to the core. Drop them into another pan of cold water, drain them, and put them into a thin syrup boiled to the "Small Thread" (215° F.). Remove the scum, and finish as for Greengages.

PINEAPPLE CHIPS (*See* Pineapple, Preserved)

PINEAPPLES, CRYSTALLIZED

Choose 1 or 2 fine pineapples, cut off the top and the stalk, and pare the rind outside the pine. Then prick to the core with a large needle in several places. Place the pine in a pan with plenty of water, boil until tender, and finish the preparation as for Apricots, either preserved or crystallized.

PINEAPPLE, PRESERVED

Pare and slice the pineapples finely, pile on a large dish, and sprinkle each layer liberally with pounded loaf or castor sugar. Keep it in a hot closet, or put it daily for 7 or 8 days into a cool oven, turning it frequently. When quite dry, bake a few slices at a time in a moderately hot oven. When cold, pack them in air-tight boxes with paper between each layer.

PINEAPPLE, PRESERVED II

Cut the pineapples into slices ¼ of an inch in thickness, trim off the edges, and remove the hard centre part. Put these trimmings into a stewpan with sufficient water to cover them, and simmer them gently for about ½ an hour. Strain, return to the stewpan, add the sliced pines, castor or loaf sugar to taste, and simmer gently for about ½ an hour, skimming occasionally meanwhile. Pineapples thus preserved will not keep long.

Pineapple

PLUMS, CRYSTALLIZED

In crystallizing plums, proceed in the same manner as in crystallizing Greengages, taking special care that the syrup is boiled to the right "thread".

PLUMS, MIRABELLE, PRESERVED OR CRYSTALLIZED

These are also preserved in the same manner as Greengages.

PLUMS, SPICED

Prick the plums well with a fork, place them in a large jar with cinnamon, cloves and orange-rind between each layer. Cover with vinegar, and, on the following day, strain off and boil for about 10 minutes. Let it cool, pour it over the fruit, and at the end of 24 hours again strain and measure it. To each pint add 3 oz. of sugar, boil the two together for 10 minutes, pour it over the plums, and, when cold, cover closely, and store in a dry, cool place.

PLUMS, TO PRESERVE

To each lb. of plums allow 1 lb. of loaf sugar and ½ a pint of water.

Put the water and sugar into a preserving-pan and boil to a thin syrup. Remove the stalks from the plums, prick them slightly to prevent them breaking, pour over them the prepared syrup, and allow them to remain thus for 2 days. Turn the whole into a preserving-pan, boil very gently until the plums are tender, then lift them carefully into pots. Boil the syrup to the "Large Thread" degree (217° F.), pour it over the plums, cover closely, and store in a cool, dry place.

PLUMS, TO PRESERVE DRY

Take an equal weight of plums and loaf sugar.

Put half the sugar into a preserving-pan with the addition of ½ a pint of cold water to each lb. of sugar, and boil to a thin syrup. Divide the plums, remove the stones, and put the fruit into the prepared syrup. Simmer gently until half-cooked, then turn the whole into an earthenware bowl, cover, and let it remain thus until the following day. Strain the syrup into a preserving-pan, add the rest of the sugar, and boil to the "Large Pearl" degree (222° F.). Allow it to cool slightly, put in the plums, simmer very gently until tender, then remove them very carefully to a deep dish and strain the syrup over them. Let the plums remain covered for 48 hours, drain well, spread them on large dishes in single layers, and when quite dry pack them in air-tight tins with wax paper between the layers.

Plums

PUMPKIN, TO PRESERVE

To each lb. of pumpkin allow 1 lb. of preserving sugar, 2 tablespoonfuls of lemon-juice, the finely-grated rind of 1 lemon, and ½ a teaspoonful of ground ginger.

Pare and halve the pumpkin, remove the seeds, and slice thinly. Lay the slices on a large dish, covering each layer thickly with sugar, add the lemon-juice, and let it remain for 3 days. Turn the whole into a preserving-pan, add the lemon-rind and ginger, and ½ a pint of cold water to 3 lb. of fruit, bring slowly to boiling-point, and continue the cooking until the slices of pumpkin are quite tender, but not broken. Transfer carefully to an earthenware bowl, let it remain covered for 7 days, then lift the slices of pumpkin carefully into jars, and strain the syrup into a preserving-pan. Boil the syrup to the "Large Pearl" degree (222° F.), pour it over the pumpkin, cover closely, and when cold, put the jars into a cool, dry place.

QUINCES, TO PRESERVE

Quince

Pare, quarter, core the quinces, and preserve the skins and cores. Put the fruit into the preserving-pan with barely enough water to cover them, and simmer until soft, but not broken. Place the quinces singly on large dishes, add the cores and parings to the water in which the quinces were cooked, and simmer gently for about 1 hour. Strain through a jelly-bag until quite clear, return it to the pan with the addition of 1 lb. of sugar for each lb. of fruit, bring to boiling-point, and skim well. Put in the quinces, boil for about 15 minutes, then turn the whole carefully into an earthenware bowl, and let the preparation remain until the following day. Drain the syrup once more into the pan; when boiling add the fruit, cook gently for 15 minutes or so, then lift the quinces carefully into small jars, which they should three-quarters fill. Continue boiling the syrup until it forms a thick jelly when tested on a cold plate, pour it over the fruit, cover the jars closely with paper brushed over on each side with white of egg, and store in a cool, dry place.

STRAWBERRIES, TO PRESERVE

Strawberries for preserving must be very dry, otherwise they will not keep; the stalks must be removed, and any unsound fruit rejected.

Take an equal weight of fruit and loaf sugar. Put the sugar into a preserving-pan; to each lb. add ½ a pint of cold water and a small pinch of cream of tartar, and boil to the "Small Ball" degree (237° F.). Now put in the prepared fruit, cover the pan, allow it to remain on the stove, but as far away from the fire as possible, for about 1 hour, then bring the contents to boiling-point and skim well. Boil gently for a few minutes, then turn into jars, cover closely, and store in a cool, dry place.

STRAWBERRIES, TO PRESERVE II

To each lb. of fruit allow 1 lb. of preserving sugar and ¼ of a pint of red-currant juice. (*See* Red-Currant Jelly.)

Pick the strawberries, pile them on a large dish, sprinkle on them half the sugar, and let them remain thus until the following day. Prepare the red-currant juice as directed, put it into a preserving-pan with the rest of the sugar, and boil to a thin syrup. Turn the fruit and syrup into the juice, and boil gently until the syrup sets quickly when tested on a cold plate. Pour gently into pots, cover with paper coated on both sides with white of egg, and keep in a cool, dry place.

Drying fruit and vegetables

Fruit is dried on drying trays and on sticks so cut as to fit on the ledges that support the oven trays.

Stilleben mit Gebäck und Zuckerwerk [Still Life with Pastry and Sweetmeats] by Georg Flegel (1566-1638)

CHAPTER VI

BOTTLING FRUIT

The bottled preserve

About 48 hours after bottling, each bottle should be held upside down (when screw-on tops are used). Should any moisture exude, the bottle is not airtight and the contents must be emptied out and re-sterilised. Bottles and jars should be clearly labelled, and the date when filled clearly stated.

BOTTLING is one of the easiest and most simple methods of preserving fruit and vegetables - especially when one possesses a proper bottling outfit, which consists of a sterilizer fitted with a thermometer to gauge the temperature of the water and bottles or jars fitted with vacuum or screw-top air-tight lids, preferably of glass - but satisfactory results may be obtained with an ordinary boiling-pot and wide-necked bottles or jars.

The bottles must be scrupulously clean and the fruit in perfectly sound, dry, and not over-ripe condition. The fruit or vegetables should be cleaned and prepared as directed in the respective recipes. Pack the fruit as tightly as possible in the bottles, cover with water and cork or put on the lids, but not too tightly. (Don't put on rubber bands.)

A little salt or a pinch of alum may be added to harden the fruit or vegetables; the addition of a piece of loaf sugar will preserve their colour.

If an ordinary boiling-pot is used for the process of sterilization, place some pieces of wood or a layer of straw at the bottom, wrap a little of the straw round each bottle to prevent contact with each other and stand them in the boiling vessel. Surround with cold water to about three-quarters of their depth and bring the water very slowly to about 170° F., taking about 1½ hours in the process. Then move the pot slightly towards the side of the stove, or reduce the heat a little and decrease the temperature very gradually about 10 to 15 degrees. The water in the pot should remain at this heat from 2 to 3 hours according to the kind of fruit being used, e.g. whether soft or hard and tough. Next remove the jars one at a time from the sterilizer, put on the rubber bands and readjust the lids and immediately return the jars to the hot water, where they should be left for another 5 minutes. Remove jars and stand them on a cloth or wooden board. Some fruits retain their colour best when bottled without water being added, while others are bottled in their syrup. (See recipes.)

After 48 hours, remove the metal clips and lift the bottles by the tops: if no moisture exudes the bottles are air-tight; if not, the fruit must be re-sterilized.

These are general instructions for bottling fruit, and applicable, in the main, to all varieties. Certain fruit, however, requires specific treatment, the directions for which space will not allow to be included here, but these special details will be found under the particular recipe.

Vegetables require blanching, i.e. boiling, for a few minutes before they are sterilized; they are then plunged into cold water and when cold packed in the bottles.

For the various methods of covering and making the bottles air-tight, see Chapter I.

Preparing the vegetables

The vegetables should be perfectly sound and not over-ripe. They must be cleaned, dried and prepared as described in the respective recipes.

Packing the fruit or vegetables

Carefully grade the fruit or vegetables and keep those of similar size together. Next pack the vegetables tightly and evenly in the bottles, using the handle of a wooden spoon. Care must be taken not to bruise the preserves.

APRICOTS, BOTTLED

Choose some firm, yellow apricots - not too ripe. Cut them in half, and take out the stones. Blanch them in boiling water until tender, then drop them into cold water. Next peel them, and put them in bottles. Break the stones and extract the kernels, blanch and add a few of the kernels. Then fill the bottles three-quarters full with syrup, cork, and finish as for Cherries, Bottled.

Cherries

CHERRIES, RED, BOTTLED

Procure some fine Kentish cherries, cut off the stalks, and put them in bottles. Choose wide-mouthed bottles, and see that they are perfectly clean and dry. Next prepare a syrup. Take 1 lb. of cane loaf sugar, dissolve it in a quart of water, and fill the bottles about three-quarters up with it. Then cork, tying the corks down with wire or string. Place the bottles upright in a copper or large saucepan, with cold water up to their necks, and gradually heat them to the first boiling. Withdraw from the fire, and let the fruit stand in the copper till next day. Then take the bottles out, clean them, cover the mouths with bottle-wax, pack in straw with the corks downwards, and store in a dry place.

CHERRIES, UNSWEETENED, BOTTLED

Procure some Kentish cherries, stone them, and put them into bottles. Cork them, and gradually heat up to about 200°. Withdraw from the fire, and finish in the same way as with other bottled fruits.

CURRANTS, BOTTLED

Choose some fine currants, pick them over, and put them in bottles. Cork, and proceed as for unsweetened Cherries.

DAMSONS, BOTTLED

Remove the stalks but not the stones, place the fruit in wide-necked glass bottles, and tie a piece of bladder securely over the top of each one. Cover the bottom of a large boiling-pot with a thin layer of straw, stand the bottles side by side on the top of it, and surround them with cold water. Bring slowly to boiling-point, then remove the boiling-pot from the fire, but let the bottles remain in it until the contents are perfectly cold. Before storing them remove the bladder, fill the mouths of the bottles with sugar, and cork with tight-fitting corks. Seal with wax, and store in a cool, dry place.

DAMSONS (OR PLUMS), BOTTLED (WITHOUT SUGAR)

Let the fruit be dry and sound. Place it in wide-necked jars, cover completely with boiling water, and pour over a good layer of melted mutton suet. Cover with parchment to exclude the air completely. The fruit will keep a considerable time, and when required for use the water should be poured off, and the jelly at the bottom of the jar used to improve the flavour of the fruit.

FRUIT, FRESH, TO BOTTLE, WITH SUGAR

Allow 4 oz. of preserving sugar to each quart of fruit, and follow the directions given under Gooseberries, Bottled.

GOOSEBERRIES, BOTTLED (WITHOUT SUGAR)

Procure some firm, sound, unripe green gooseberries.

Head and tail them, put into wide-necked glass bottles, cover with water and secure the lids. Wrap a little hay or straw round each bottle. Put a thin layer of the same on the bottom of a large boiling-pot, stand the bottles on the top of it, and surround them to at least three-quarters of their depth with cold water. Bring the water slowly to boiling-point, then remove the pan from the fire, but allow the bottles to remain in it until the gooseberries begin to rise in them. Now add to each one a little boiling water, cork with new corks, and cover the bottles with bladder. Place them on their sides in a cool, dry place.

GOOSEBERRIES, BOTTLED (WITH SUGAR)

To each lb. of firm, sound, green gooseberries allow 1 lb. of loaf or granulated sugar and ½ a pint of water.

Head and tail the gooseberries, cover them with cold water, simmer slowly until tender, but unbroken, then drain well, and put them into cold water. Dissolve the sugar in the water, boil to a syrup, then let it become quite cold. Drain the gooseberries well, put them into the cold syrup, bring to boiling-point, boil gently for 10 minutes, then turn the whole into an earthenware bowl. Next day drain the syrup into a preserving-pan or large stewpan, boil it to the "large thread" degree (217° F.), then put in the fruit and boil gently for about 10 minutes. Turn into hot, dry bottles, cork securely with new corks, and cover the tops with bladder.

GREENGAGES, BOTTLED

Proceed as for Apricots.

MIRABELLE PLUMS, BOTTLED

Choose some fine mirabelle plums - not too ripe. Prick them, and drop them into boiling water for a few minutes; then take them out with a skimmer, and drop them into cold water. Strain, and put them into bottles, add the syrup, and finish as for other fruits.

PEACHES, BOTTLED

The method is the same as for Apricots, Bottled.

RASPBERRIES, BOTTLED

Proceed as for Gooseberries, Bottled.

STRAWBERRIES, ETC., BOTTLED

For each of these preserves proceed in the same way as for all other fruits of this kind, taking care that the fruit, in each case, is sound, and not too ripe.

Bottles for preserving

Preserving bottles or jars are made with vacuum or screw-top airtight lids - preferably of glass. These two illustrations show how the lids are adjusted.

Before use the bottles and jars must be carefully sterilised by being well washed, dried, and then made very hot in the oven.

Sterilisers

A sterilising apparatus is essential if much bottling is to be done. The water should three-quarter cover the bottles; make sure also that the water covers the thermometer bulb.

Sterilisers make the bottling of preserves a very simple matter. If, however, you do not possess a steriliser, an ordinary boiling pot will serve the purpose, but the jars must be wrapped in cloths or straw to prevent them from damaging each other.

Strawberries, Nuts, and Citrus by Raphaelle Peale (1822)

CHAPTER VII

FRUITS IN BRANDY

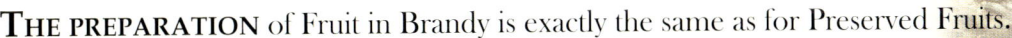

THE PREPARATION of Fruit in Brandy is exactly the same as for Preserved Fruits.

All fruits containing pectin or vegetable jelly, such as apricots, red cherries, greengages, mogul plums, peaches, etc., may be preserved in brandy. Care should be taken to select suitable fruits, viz., those which are firm, and not too ripe. Fruits that are too ripe will not keep, and soon become mashed to a marmalade in the bottles.

APRICOTS IN BRANDY

Take some fine yellow apricots - not too ripe - prick them over, then blanch them in boiling water until they are soft, but not too tender. When the apricots rise to the surface, drop them in cold water, drain them on a sieve, and prepare a plain syrup. Put in the apricots and let them boil, remove from the fire, and mix to every pint of syrup 2 pints of best brandy. Put the apricots into clean, dry bottles, and pour over the liquor. When cold, make the bottles air-tight.

BLACK CURRANTS IN BRANDY

Take some fine black currants, pick, and wash them in cold water. Drain them on a sieve. Have ready some cherry brandy, and add the black currants. Boil gently for a few minutes, remove from the fire, and bottle when cold.

CHERRIES IN BRANDY

Take some fine morello cherries. Remove the stems, then drop them into cold water. Wash them well, drain them on a sieve, and put them into clean, dry bottles. Next pour over sufficient brandy to cover them, add a little cinnamon, make the bottles air-tight, and allow them to remain for a month. Then drain off the brandy, and to each pint add 4 oz. of castor sugar. Mix well and melt it, then strain the liquor through flannel until it is bright and clear, and pour this over the cherries. They are then ready for use.

GREENGAGES IN BRANDY

Take some fine greengages - not too ripe - prick them with a fork, put them into a pan of water with a little alum in it, and set the pan over the fire. When tender, put them into cold water, and let them stand for 2 hours. Prepare a plain syrup, and finish as for Apricots in Brandy.

MIRABELLE PLUMS IN BRANDY

Prepare in the same way as Apricots in Brandy.

MOGUL PLUMS IN BRANDY

Mogul plums are prepared in the same way as Apricots in Brandy.

ORANGES IN BRANDY

Choose some fine large oranges, put them into a pan of hot water, and boil until tender. Then drop them into cold water, and drain them. Prepare a plain syrup. Put the oranges in it, and let them boil for about 5 minutes. Remove from the fire, and finish as for Apricots in Brandy.

PEACHES IN BRANDY

Proceed as for Apricots in Brandy, taking care not to bruise or crush the fruit.

PEARS IN BRANDY

Take some fine large eating pears - not too ripe or juicy - prick them all over, blanch them until soft, and then drop them into cold water. Pare off the rind very thinly, prick the pears well with a bodkin, and drop them into another pan of cold water. Put the pan on the fire again until the fruit is thoroughly scalded, or blanched, and can easily be run through with a bodkin or pin's head. Put them again into cold water, drain, and finish as for Apricots in Brandy.

CHAPTER VIII

FRUIT PASTES AND CURDS

APPLE PASTE

Take 4 lb. of apples, boil them in water until they are soft, then mash them, and pass them through a sieve into a pan. Next, boil 4 lb. of loaf sugar to the "Small Crack" (290° F.), remove from the fire, and pour the sugar into the pan with the mashed apples. Put the pan on the fire, and stir the contents well while boiling, until it comes away from the sides of the pan. Remove the mixture from the fire, and pour it out in a thin layer on sheets of tin, powdered with sugar. Put the tin plates in an oven to dry until next day, then turn the paste over in order that it may dry both sides. When ready, take out and cut the paste into long, narrow strips. These can be shaped into knots or any other form, such as rings, leaves, bon-bons, crosses, gimlets, sticks, lozenges, etc.

Note: today this and the other dried pastes are sometimes called fruit leather.

APRICOT PASTE

Take 2 lb. of apricots. Pass them through a hair sieve, add 1 lb. of cane sugar to 1 lb. of pulp, put them on a clear fire, and stir well as they boil until the mixture leaves the bottom of the pan. Remove from the fire, and finish as for Apple Paste.

APRICOT PULP, PRESERVED

Take some fine ripe apricots, stone them, and pass them through a hair sieve into a basin. Weigh the pulp, adding to every 4 lb., 1 lb. of finely sifted castor sugar. Break the stones and take out the kernels. Blanch them, cut them in halves, and add some of them to the pulp. Put the pulp into clean, dry tin boxes, solder the lids down, then place them upright in a copper with enough cold water to cover them. Put the copper on the fire and boil up well, then withdraw from the fire and let them stand until the next day. When quite cold, take out, and store in a dry place until required.

BLACK-CURRANT PASTE

Pass the currants through a hair sieve. Put them into a pan and boil for about 15 minutes. Remove the pan from the fire, and weigh the pulp. Add 1 lb. of cane loaf sugar to each lb. of pulp, mix well, and finish as for other pastes.

DAMSON CHEESE

Remove the stalks from the damsons, and put the fruit into a large jar or stew-pot. Cover closely, cook in a very slow oven until perfectly soft, then rub through a fine sieve. Measure the pulp, and put it into a preserving-pan with the addition of 12 or 16 oz. of sugar to each pint of pulp, according to individual taste. Boil until the greater part of the syrup has evaporated and the pulp has become rather stiff, stirring frequently at first and almost continuously towards the end of the process. Turn into small jars, cover closely, and store in a cool, dry place. The stones may be cracked and the kernels added to the puree with the sugar.

DAMSON CHEESE II

After removing the stalks from the damsons, put the fruit into a large jar placed in a boiling-pot of cold water, and cook until perfectly soft. Now take away the stones, pour off some of the juice, which should afterwards be converted into damson jelly, and add from 6 to 8 oz. of sugar to each lb. of fruit. Continue the slow cooking for about 2 hours longer, then turn the whole into a preserving-pan, and boil rapidly for about ½ an hour, meanwhile stirring continuously. Turn into small pots, cover closely, and store in a cool, dry place.

Damsons

DAMSON PASTE

Proceed exactly as in making Apricot Paste.

GREENGAGE PASTE

Greengage Paste is made in the same manner as Apricot Paste, both as regards the proportions of fruit, and sugar, and the method of preparation.

GREENGAGE PULP, PRESERVED

Here again the process is as in preparing Apricot Pulp.

LEMON CURD

Take 4 eggs, 1 lb. of castor sugar, 4 oz. of butter and the rind and juice of 4 lemons.

Break the eggs separately into a basin, beat slightly, add the other ingredients and stir over a gentle heat in a pan of hot water for about 20 minutes, or until thick. Pour into dry jars, cover down securely, and store in a cold, dry place.

MIRABELLE PASTE

Mirabelle Paste is made in every respect in the same way as Apricot Paste.

MIRABELLE PULP, PRESERVED

Proceed as in the preparation of Apricot Pulp.

PEACH PASTE

Peach Paste is prepared in the same manner as Apricot Paste. Success will depend greatly upon the sugar being heated to the right degree.

PEACH PULP, PRESERVED

The process is again as in preparing Apricot Pulp. Especial care in choosing the peaches is required.

PLUM PASTE

Plum Paste also is made like Apricot Paste, the fruit being passed through a hair sieve, and the process finished as in preparing Apple Paste.

QUINCE PASTE

Quince Paste is prepared in exactly the same way as Apple Paste, substituting quinces for apples.

RED-CURRANT PASTE

Prepare in the same manner as Black-Currant Paste.

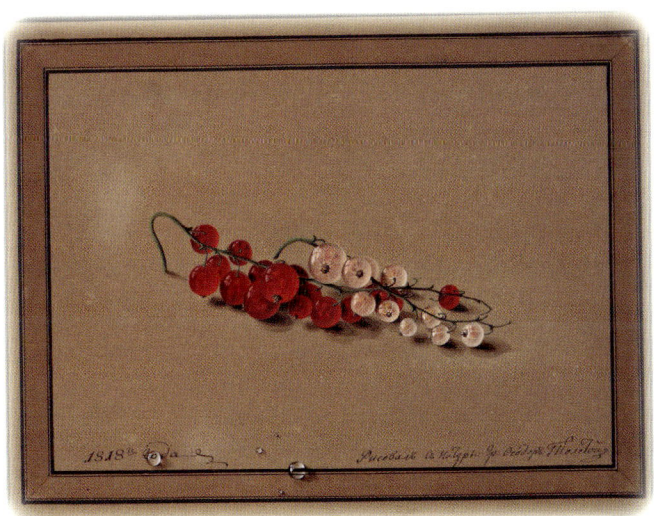

Berries of Red and White Currant by Fyodor Petrovich Tolstoy (1818)

Fruit Pastes and Curds

Crab apples by Louise Blakeney (1903)

CHAPTER IX

SYRUPS AND FRUIT JUICES

THE aim in preparing syrups is to preserve the aroma or flavour of the fruits, flowers, or vegetables from which they are extracted.

The best syrups should be made with the finest refined cane sugar only, and with the best fruits, etc. Inferior sugar, as well as over-ripe fruits, often cause sediments, or fermentation in the syrups.

The principal points or degrees to which syrups should be boiled, are from the "small thread" (215° F.) to the "large pearl" (222° F.); for if insufficiently boiled, the syrup is apt to become cloudy and mouldy, and if over-boiled it will become candied.

Great care should therefore be taken to boil the syrup to the precise point. If it should, accidentally, be boiled too much, and to too high a degree, add a little water and boil up again.

Note that all fruits containing pectin or vegetable jelly require to stand - after being mashed - for about 2 or 3 days, in order to ferment, and to prevent the syrup from becoming jelly when bottled.

ALMOND SYRUP

Take 1 lb. of sweet almonds and 4 oz. of bitter almonds, blanch, and wash them in clean water. Put them into a mortar and pound finely. Add the juice of 2 lemons, 1 oz. of gum arabic, and ½ a pint of water. When the almonds are reduced to a fine paste, add another ½ pint of water, then pass through a sieve into a clean basin, and add 2 lb. of the best cane sugar. Boil the syrup for a few minutes after the sugar is dissolved, withdraw from the fire, and remove the scum. Stir the syrup until cold, strain through a jelly-bag, and add a little orange-flower water, then bottle and tie down.

CURRANT SYRUP

Take some fresh, ripe currants, either white or red, pick them over, mash them in a basin and let them stand for 2 or 3 days. Strain the juice through a flannel jelly-bag. Take 4 lb. of the best refined cane sugar, and let it dissolve in 1 quart of currant juice. Finish as for Raspberry Syrup.

Note: Some confectioners take the following fruit for making currant syrup: 5 lb. of red currants, 3 lb. of stoned cherries, and 1 lb. of raspberries; mix, mash, and leave to ferment for 2 or 3 days.

GINGER SYRUP

Make a pint of plain syrup, and pour in a few drops of essence of ginger: add a little caramel colouring. Bottle when cold and tie down.

LEMON SYRUP

Take ½ a pint of plain syrup, and a gill of lemon-juice.

Let the juice settle, take off the thin skin which forms on the top, then strain through a jelly-bag. Now pour the lemon juice into the syrup, gently boil it to the "Large Pearl" (222° F.), and remove the scum. Strain through a flannel bag until clear. When cold, bottle and tie down.

MAIDENHAIR SYRUP

Take 2 oz. of capillaire [dried maidenhair fern leaves], cut up into little pieces, then infuse them in 1½ pints of boiling water, covering the pan over. After 2 hours' infusion strain it through a cloth, add 2 lb. of the best cane sugar, and the white of an egg beaten up. Boil to the "Large Pearl" (222° F.), then strain through a flannel until clear. Bottle when cold and tie down.

MORELLO CHERRY SYRUP

Take 4 lb. of the cane sugar, dissolve it in 1 quart of cherry juice, and proceed as in making Raspberry Syrup.

MULBERRY SYRUP

Take 5 lb. of the best cane sugar, dissolve it in 3 pints of mulberry juice, and finish as in making Raspberry Syrup.

ORANGE SYRUP

Proceed as for Lemon Syrup, substituting oranges instead of the lemons.

ORANGE-FLOWER SYRUP

Take 1 pint of plain syrup, boil it to the "Small Crack" (290° F.), then pour in ½ a pint of orange-flower water. Boil for a minute or so, remove the scum, and then finish as for Lemon Syrup.

Ginger

PLAIN SYRUP I

Take 1 lb. of refined cane sugar, dissolve it in ½ a pint of water, boil for a few minutes after the sugar is dissolved, withdraw from the fire, and remove the scum. Boil up again to the "Large Pearl" (222° F.), remove, and strain through a flannel bag until clear. When cold, bottle and tie down.

PLAIN SYRUP II

Take 1 lb. of loaf sugar, dissolve it in ½ a pint of water, and boil for a few minutes after the sugar is dissolved. Withdraw from the fire and remove the scum. Put on the fire again, boil for another minute or so, and remove the scum. This produces a syrup equal to about the "Small Thread" (215° F.).

RASPBERRY SYRUP

Take plenty of fresh raspberries, either white or red, pick them over, mash them in a basin, and let them stand for 2 or 3 days. Strain the juice through a flannel jelly-bag. Take 4 lb. of the best cane sugar, and let it dissolve in 1 quart of raspberry juice, put the syrup on the fire, and boil for a few minutes. After the sugar is dissolved, withdraw from the fire and remove the scum. Boil up again to the "Large Pearl" (222° F.), remove from the fire, and strain through a flannel bag until clear. Bottle when cold, and tie down with corks or bladder.

STRAWBERRY SYRUP

Proceed as in making Raspberry Syrup, substituting strawberries instead of the raspberries.

UNSWEETENED FRUIT JUICE FOR ICES

The juice of raspberries, strawberries, cherries, and red currants may be preserved by boiling the juice in bottles for about 20 minutes in the same way as for unsweetened bottled fruits. The sugar can be added afterwards, or when the juice is wanted for use.

Strawberries

Maidenhair Fern

Syrups and Fruit Juices

Still-Life with Cherries, Strawberries and Gooseberries by Louise Moillon (1630)

CHAPTER X

PICKLES

PICKLES may now be purchased in such variety and so cheaply that very few, save those who grow vegetables they cannot utilize in any other way, think of preparing them at home. Pickles consist of vegetables and fruits steeped in vinegar previously boiled with spices, to which is frequently added salt and sugar, in quantities varied according to individual taste. The chief pickles are cabbage, cauliflower, chillies, gherkins, onions, and walnuts. Any or all of these, except cabbage, may be mixed. Indian pickles form a class by themselves; they are generally thick and highly spiced, mangoes forming a general base.

To make pickles successfully, the vegetables or fruit must be perfectly dry, fresh; and not over-ripe; strong vinegar and fresh spices are essential.

The vinegar must not be over-boiled as it then loses its preserving properties; the vegetables, once cut up, should be used immediately.

No pickles or chutneys are at their best until they have been allowed to mature for at least 3 months. They must be covered and tied down while hot.

ADULTERATION IN PICKLES

Sulphuric acid is often present in vinegar in a larger amount than the law allows [not a problem today], i.e., 1 part in 1,000, and it is very injurious to health even in a small amount.

Pickles sometimes contain copper, added in order to fix the chlorophyll, or green colouring matter, in the vegetables. Most authorities consider it poisonous; its presence may be detected by a coppery tinge imparted to the silver with which it comes in contact. If available, vinegar should be boiled in an enamelled pan, or, failing this, a stew-jar placed in a saucepan of boiling water. If a metal pan must of necessity be used, one made of iron produces the least injurious effects. Fatal results have followed the use of copper vessels for pickling purposes [this is a very important warning]. As far as possible avoid the use of metal in the preparation of pickles.

BRINE FOR PICKLING

Fruit and vegetables are often pickled in brine. This may be made by mixing salt, vinegar and water in the proportion of: salt, 8 oz.; vinegar, ½ pint; and water, 1½ pints. Heat until salt is dissolved; cool and use clear solution only.

APPLE CHUTNEY

Have ready 2¼ lb. of thickly-sliced apples, 1 lb. of brown sugar, ¾ of a lb. of sultanas, ½ oz. of salt, ½ an oz. of mustard seeds, ½ an oz. of ground ginger, ¼ of an oz. of garlic bruised, $\frac{1}{8}$ of an oz. of cayenne and 1 pint of good vinegar.

Simmer the vinegar, sugar and apples gently until reduced to a pulp, stir in the remaining ingredients, and, when well mixed, turn the whole into a basin. Cover, stir two or three times daily for 1 week, then bottle, and cork securely.

ARTICHOKES, PICKLED

Artichoke

Make a strong brine; when boiling put in the Globe artichokes, boil gently for 10 or 15 minutes, and drain well. Remove and put aside the chokes, place the artichokes in jars, and cover them with boiling spiced vinegar. When cold, fill the jars with salad-oil, cover closely, and store.

BEETROOT PICKLE

Procure 6 medium-sized beetroots, 1 quart of malt vinegar, ½ an oz. of whole black pepper, ½ an oz. of allspice, 1 small horseradish grated and salt to taste.

Wash the beetroots well, taking care not to break the skins, and bake them in a moderate oven for about 1½ hours. When cool enough to handle remove the skins, cut the beetroots into ½-inch slices, and place them in jars. Meanwhile boil the vinegar, horseradish, pepper and spice together, let the mixture become quite cold, then pour in over the beetroot. Cover the jars closely with parchment paper coated on both sides with white of egg, and store in a cool, dry place.

BEETROOT PICKLE II

Take 6 beetroots, 1 quart of vinegar, ½ an oz. of whole pepper and ½ an oz. of allspice.

Wash the beetroots well, but take care to keep the skins intact, or they will lose some of their colouring matter. Put them into boiling water, cook gently for about 1½ hours, until they are three-quarters cooked, then drain them, and let them cool. Boil the spice, pepper and vinegar together, and put these aside until quite cold, meanwhile peel the beetroots, cut them into ½-inch slices, and place them in jars. Pour the cold prepared vinegar over them, cover closely, and store in a cool, dry place. The pickle will be ready for use in 1 week.

BLUEBERRIES, OR BILBERRIES, PICKLED (*See* Currants, Spiced and Cherries, Pickled)

CABBAGE, PICKLED RED

Procure 1 good firm red cabbage, 1 quart of vinegar, ½ an oz. of whole pepper and ½ an oz. of allspice.

Remove the outer leaves of the cabbage, quarter it, remove the centre stalk, and cut each section across into very fine strips. Pile the shredded cabbage on a large dish, sprinkle it liberally with salt, and let it remain thus until the following day. Meanwhile boil the vinegar, pepper and spice together, the latter being tied together in a piece of muslin, and allow the preparation to become quite cold. Turn the cabbage into an earthenware or enamelled colander, and when well drained put it into a large jar, and pour in the vinegar. It will be fit for use in 3 or 4 days; if kept for any length of time the cabbage loses the crispness and colour which are its chief recommendations.

Red cabbage

CABBAGE, PICKLED RED II

Take 1 good cabbage, 1 quart of malt vinegar, ½ an oz. of black peppercorns and ½ an oz. of allspice.

Remove the outer leaves of the cabbage, quarter it, cut away the stalk from the centre, and shred the sections across as finely as possible. Put the prepared cabbage into a large jar, sprinkle each layer with salt, and press the whole lightly down. Boil the pepper and spice in the vinegar; when cold, pour it over the jars, and cover them closely. The pickle will be ready for use in 3 or 4 days; it may be kept for a considerable time, but after being pickled for 2 or 3 weeks it loses much of its crispness and colour.

CAPSICUMS, PICKLED

If the capsicums can be obtained from the garden, they should be gathered when they are just at the point of turning red. To each quart of vinegar allow 1 teaspoonful of salt, and ½ a teaspoonful of mace and nutmeg mixed in equal proportions. Slit the capsicums at the side, take out the seeds, put the capsicums into a jar, and sprinkle over them the salt, mace and nutmeg. Boil the vinegar, pour it at once upon the pods, and, when cold, cover closely with parchment paper or bladder. They will be ready for use in 4 or 5 weeks.

CAPSICUMS, PICKLED II

Have ready some young green capsicums and to each quart of vinegar allow 1 teaspoonful of salt and ½ a teaspoonful of ground mace.

Remove the stalks, scald the capsicums, and let them remain under pressure for 24 hours, to extract some of their bitter water. Pack the capsicums closely in a jar, pour over

Cauliflower

them boiling vinegar seasoned with salt and mace, and, when quite cold, cover closely. They will be ready for use in 5 or 6 weeks.

CAULIFLOWERS, PICKLED

Select firm white cauliflowers and procure sufficient vinegar to cover them. To each quart of vinegar allow 1 teaspoonful of peppercorns, 1 teaspoonful of allspice and 6 cloves.

Break the cauliflowers into small sprays, place them on a dish, sprinkle them liberally with salt, and let them remain thus for 6 hours. Meanwhile tie the seasoning ingredients in muslin, boil them in the vinegar for about ½ an hour, and allow it to become quite cold. Drain the cauliflowers well from the salt, place them in wide-necked bottles or unglazed jars, and pour the prepared vinegar over them. Cover closely, store in a cool, dry place for about 1 month.

CAULIFLOWERS, PICKLED II

Procure some firm white cauliflowers and sufficient vinegar to cover them. To each quart of vinegar allow 1 teaspoonful of peppercorns, 1 teaspoonful of allspice.

Tie the peppercorns and allspice in muslin, simmer these very gently in the vinegar for about 20 minutes, and put aside until quite cold. Have ready a saucepan of boiling, highly-salted water, break the cauliflowers into small sprays, throw them into the water, boil for 5 minutes, and drain well. When quite cold put them into wide-necked bottles or unglazed jars, with a few peppercorns and a little allspice, cover with the prepared vinegar, and cover closely. They should be ready for use in 3 or 4 weeks.

CAULIFLOWERS, PICKLED, WITH ONIONS

Take an equal weight of cauliflower sprays and silver-onions, and procure sufficient vinegar to cover. To each quart of vinegar allow 1 level teaspoonful of peppercorns, 1 level teaspoonful of allspice, 1 level teaspoonful of black pepper, 1 blade of mace, 1 oz. of turmeric, 1 tablespoonful of curry-powder, 1 tablespoonful of dry mustard, 1 tablespoonful of salt, 1 tablespoonful of lemon-juice, and about 1 tablespoonful of raw lime-juice.

Put as much water as will cover the sprays of cauliflower into a large saucepan; to each quart add 4 oz. of salt, boil for 10 minutes, and allow it to become quite cold. Break the cauliflowers into small sprays, cover them with the cold brine, let them remain immersed for 3 days, then drain well. Peel the onions, place them in jars or wide-necked bottles in layers alternating with sprays of cauliflower; sprinkle each layer with a little allspice, a few peppercorns, and 1 or 2 pieces of mace. Mix the black pepper, turmeric, curry-powder, mustard and salt, lemon-juice and lime-juice, to a smooth paste, add the vinegar gradually to the paste, and pour the whole over the cauliflowers and onions. Cover closely, and store in a cool, dry place. The pickle will be ready for use in 3 or 4 weeks.

CHERRIES, PICKLED

Select some sound, not over-ripe cherries and procure sufficient French vinegar to cover them. To each pint of vinegar allow ½ a lb. of sugar, and to the whole add cayenne to taste. A few drops of cochineal or carmine for colouring.

Pick the cherries carefully, rejecting those which are not quite sound, leave about 1 inch of their stalks, and put the fruit into jars. Boil the vinegar, add to it the sugar and cayenne, skim well, let it boil for a few minutes, then turn it into an earthenware vessel. When cold, add a few drops of carmine or cochineal, pour it over the cherries, cover the jars closely, and store in a cool, dry place until required for use.

CHERRIES, PICKLED II

Take some sound, not over-ripe cherries and sufficient good vinegar to cover them. To each quart of vinegar allow 1 lb. of sugar.

Leave 1 inch of the stalks on the cherries, and pack them lightly in jars. Boil the vinegar and sugar together, pour it whilst hot over the fruit, and when cold tie paper over the jars. Let them stand in a cool place for 1 week, then drain off the vinegar, boil and skim well, and again pour while hot over the fruit. When cold cover closely, and keep in a cool, dry place.

CHUTNEY, APPLE (*See* Apple Chutney)

CHUTNEY, ENGLISH

Have ready 3 dozen sour apples, 3 lb. of coarse brown sugar, ⅓ a lb. of salt, 2 lb. of sultana raisins, ½ a lb. of green ginger, 6 oz. of bird's-eye chillies, 2 oz. of mustard-seed, 5 medium sized Spanish onions, 6 shallots and 3 quarts of good malt vinegar.

Dissolve the salt and sugar in the vinegar, strain, and return it to the stewpan. Add the apples, onions and ginger, all thinly sliced, the sultanas cleaned and picked, also the rest of the ingredients, and cook very gently until the apples and onions are quite tender. Pour into small jars or wide-necked bottles; when cold, cover closely, and store in a cool, dry place.

CHUTNEY, INDIAN

Take 1 quart of malt vinegar, 1 lb. of sour apples, peeled, cored and sliced, ½ a lb. of onions, peeled and coarsely chopped, 1 lb. of moist sugar, ½ a lb. of raisins stoned and quartered. 4 oz. of salt, 4 oz. of ground ginger, 2 oz. of dry mustard, ¼ of an oz. of cayenne and 4 small cloves of garlic finely chopped.

Cook the apples, onions and garlic with the salt, sugar and vinegar until quite soft, and pass them through a fine hair sieve. Add the raisins, ginger, cayenne and mustard, mix well together, turn into a jar, and stand it in a warm, but not hot, place until the following day. Have ready some perfectly dry, wide-necked small bottles or jars, fill them with chutney, and cover closely so as to exclude the air. This chutney may be kept for a year or two.

CHUTNEY, MANGO

To 50 green mangoes allow 6 pints of vinegar, 3 lb. of sugar, 2 lb. of tamarinds stoned, 1 lb. of raisins stoned, 1 lb. of green ginger sliced, 1 good teaspoonful of powdered cinnamon, 1 level teaspoonful of nutmeg and 1 lb. of salt.

Peel and slice the mangoes thinly, sprinkle over them the salt, let them remain for 36 hours, then drain well. Make a syrup by boiling together 3 pints of vinegar and the sugar. Put the remainder of the vinegar into a preserving-pan, add the mangoes, boil up, simmer gently for about 10 minutes, then add the tamarinds, raisins, ginger, cinnamon and nutmeg. Cook very slowly for about ½ an hour, adding the syrup gradually during the last 10 minutes. Stir and boil the mixture until the greater part of the syrup is absorbed, then turn into bottles, cork securely, and store in a cool, dry place until required for use.

CHUTNEY SAUCE, INDIAN

Mix together in a jar 4 oz. of sour apples, pared, cored and sliced, 4 oz. of tomatoes sliced, 4 oz. of salt, 4 oz. of brown sugar, 4 oz. of raisins stoned, 2 oz. of cayenne, 2 oz. of ground ginger, 1 oz. of shallots, ¼ of an oz. of garlic, 3 pints of malt vinegar and 1 pint of lemon-juice.

Cover the jar, keep in a moderately warm place for 1 month, and stir two or three times daily. At the end of the time strain off the liquor, let the residue drain well, but do not squeeze it. Pour into small bottles, cork tightly, and store in a cool, dry place.

CHUTNEY, TOMATO

Take 6 lb. of ripe tomatoes, 3 lb. of sour cooking apples, 4 oz. of salt, 8 oz. of brown sugar, 3 pints of vinegar, 6 cloves of garlic, 6 oz. of ground ginger and 1 oz. of mustard-seed.

Scald the tomatoes, remove the skin, cut them into slices, and put them into an earthenware cooking-pot with the vinegar, salt and apples previously peeled, cored and chopped finely. When the fruit is soft, rub the whole through a sieve, add the sugar, ginger and mustard-seed, also the garlic (chopped finely), and boil the whole gently from ½ to ¾ of

Tomatoes

an hour. Pour the contents of the cooking-pot into a jar, cover it, and let it stand in a warm place for about 3 days. Then bottle the chutney for use, cork up tightly, and exclude the air. Sultanas or preserved ginger are sometimes added to the above ingredients.

CUCUMBERS, PICKLED

Peel the cucumbers, cut them into ½ inch slices, sprinkle them liberally with salt, and let them remain until the following day. Let the cucumber drain for at least 2 hours on a hair sieve, then place in wide-necked glass bottles. Boil sufficient good vinegar to cover them, adding to each pint of vinegar ½ an oz. of peppercorns, ½ an oz. of allspice, and ½ a teaspoonful of salt, and pour it while hot over the cucumber, and cover closely. If stored in a cool, dry place this pickle will keep good for some time, but as it is liable to become mouldy the bottles should be frequently examined. When the first speck of mould appears re-boil the vinegar, immerse the slices of cucumber in it for 1 minute, then put them into a clean dry bottle, and pour the boiling vinegar over them. [Today, we do not advise trying to rescue mouldy pickle in this way – if in doubt, throw it out!]

Cucumber

DAMSONS, PICKLED

Have ready 7 lb. of sound, dry damson plums, 4 lb. of good preserving sugar, ¾ of an oz. of stick cinnamon, ¾ of an oz. of cloves and sufficient good vinegar to cover.

Remove the stalks but not the stems of the fruit, place them in layers in a large jar, sprinkle each layer with sugar, cinnamon and cloves. Cover the whole with vinegar, place the jar in a saucepan of boiling water, cook gently until the juice flows freely, then put the jar aside until the contents are quite cold. Then drain the syrup into a stewpan, bring to boiling-point, and pour it over the fruit. Repeat this process for 7 or 8 days, when the skins should be hard and the plums have a clear appearance. After the last boiling let the plums remain in the large jar for 7 days, then transfer them to smaller jars. Boil the syrup, pour it over the plums, and when cold cover with a bladder or paper brushed over on both sides with white of egg. Cherries may be pickled in this way. If stored in a dry, moderately cool place, they may be kept for years.

ENGLISH CHUTNEY (*See* Chutney, English)

EXCELLENT PICKLE (For Immediate Use)

Place equal quantities of sliced onion, cucumber and sour apple in a dish in alternate layers, add salt and cayenne to taste. To ½ a pint of vinegar add 1 wineglassful each of sherry (optional) and soy and pour over. Let the pickle stand for a few hours before serving.

Pickles

FRENCH BEANS, PICKLED

Cover the young French beans with strong salt and water, let them remain for 3 days, then drain. Place them in a saucepan with vine leaves under and over, cover with boiling salted water, cook gently for a few minutes, then drain and pack loosely in jars. Cover with boiling spiced vinegar, drain it off, and re-boil on two following days. The pickled beans should be kept closely covered in a cool, dry place.

GHERKINS, PICKLED

Cover the gherkins with salt and water, and let them remain in the brine for 3 days. At the end of the time drain them well, dry them with a cloth, and pack them compactly in a jar of suitable size. Boil sufficient vinegar to cover them, allowing to each quart of vinegar ¼ of an oz. of allspice, ¼ of an oz. of black peppercorns, 4 cloves and 2 blades of mace, for 10 minutes and pour the liquid over the gherkins. Cover closely, let the jar stand in a warm place until the following day, then drain off the vinegar into a saucepan. Boil up, pour the vinegar at once over the gherkins, and let them remain covered until the following day. This process must be repeated daily until the gherkins are sufficiently green; they should then be put into wide-necked glass bottles, covered completely with vinegar, for which purpose it may be necessary to supplement that already used. They should be tightly corked before being stored away.

GOOSEBERRY CHUTNEY

Chop 1 quart of green gooseberries, 10 oz. of sultanas, and 1 onion; put into the preserving-pan with 1 quart of vinegar, 1½ oz. of ground ginger, 1½ oz. of mustard-seed, 3 oz. of salt, 8 oz. of sugar, ¼ oz. of cayenne and ½ oz. of turmeric. Boil gently for about ¾ of an hour, stirring occasionally. Bottle and tie down.

HORSERADISH, PICKLED

Scrape the outer skin off the horseradish, cut it into ½-inch lengths, and place them in wide-necked bottles or small unglazed jars. Cover with good malt vinegar, cork the bottles tightly or fasten parchment paper securely over the tops of the jars. Keep the pickle in a cool, dry place.

INDIAN CHUTNEY (*See* Chutney, Indian)

INDIAN MAIZE, PICKLED

Boil the corn in salt and water, drain well and cover with spiced vinegar. When cold, fasten down securely, and store in a dry, cool place.

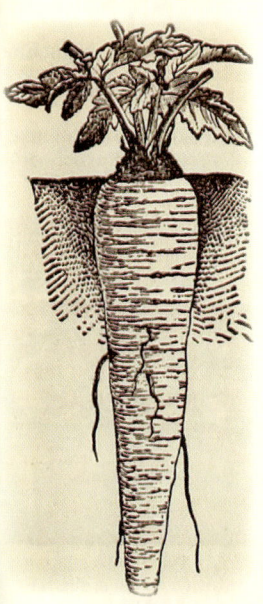

Horseradish

INDIAN PICKLE

To each gallon of vinegar allow 6 cloves of garlic, 12 shallots, 2 sticks of sliced horseradish, ¼ of a lb. of bruised ginger, 2 oz. of whole black pepper, 1 oz. of long pepper, 1 oz. of allspice, 12 cloves, ¼ of an oz. of cayenne, 2 oz. of mustard-seed, ¼ of a lb. of mustard, 1 oz. of turmeric, a white cabbage, cauliflowers, radish pods, French beans, gherkins, small round pickling onions, nasturtiums, capsicums, chillies, etc.

Nasturtium

Cut the cabbage, which must be hard and white, into slices, and the cauliflowers into small branches; sprinkle salt over them in a large dish, and let them remain for 2 days. Then dry the vegetables and put them into a very large jar, with garlic, shallots, horseradish, ginger, pepper, allspice, and cloves in the above proportions. Boil sufficient vinegar to cover the ingredients, and pour it over them, and, when cold, cover closely. As the other materials for the pickle ripen at different times, they may be added as they are ready; these will be radish pods, French beans, gherkins, small onions, nasturtiums, capsicums, chillies, etc., etc. As these are procured they must, first of all, be washed in a little cold vinegar, wiped, and then simply added to the other ingredients in the large jar, only taking care that they are covered by the vinegar. If it should be necessary to add more vinegar to the pickle, do not omit to boil it before adding it to the rest. When all the things required are collected, turn all out into a large pan, thoroughly mix them, put the mixed vegetables into smaller jars, without any of the vinegar, then boil the vinegar again, adding as much more as will be required to fill the different jars, also cayenne, mustard-seed, turmeric, and mustard, which must be well mixed with a little cold vinegar, allowing the quantities named above to each gallon of vinegar. Pour the vinegar, boiling hot, over the pickle, and, when cold, tie down with a bladder. If the pickle is wanted for immediate use, the vinegar should be boiled twice more, but the better plan is to make it during one season for use during the next. This pickle will keep for years, if care is taken that the vegetables are quite covered by the vinegar.

LEMON PICKLE

Take 12 lemons, 1 lb. of baysalt, 4 oz. of mustard-seed (tied in muslin), 2 oz. of garlic peeled, ½ an oz. of grated nutmeg, ½ an oz. of ground mace, ¼ of an oz. of ground cloves and 1 quart of white-wine vinegar.

Remove the rinds of the lemons in thin slices, and put them aside to be afterwards dried and used for flavouring purposes. Leave all the pith on the lemons, cut them lengthwise and across, thus forming 4 quarters, sprinkle over them the salt, and place them singly on a large dish. Let the dish remain near the fire until all the juice of the lemons has dried into the pith, then put them into a large jar. Add the rest of the ingredients, cover closely, and

let it stand near the fire, but not on the stove, for 5 days. At the end of the time, cover the lid with parchment paper or bladder, and put the jar in a cool, dry place. At the end of 3 months strain off the vinegar through a hair sieve, and press the fruit well to extract as much moisture as possible. Strain two or three times, and, when quite clear, bottle for use. Store in a cool, dry place.

LEMONS, PICKLED

Take 12 lemons and sufficient vinegar to cover them. To each quart of vinegar allow 1 oz. of mustard-seed, 1 oz. of whole ginger, ½ an oz. of peppercorns, about ½ an oz. of cloves, ¼ of an oz. of mace and ¼ of an oz. of chillies.

Make a brine strong enough to float an egg, put in the lemons, allow them to remain immersed for 6 days, stirring them two or three times daily. At the end of this time, put the lemons into a saucepan of boiling water, boil steadily for about 15 minutes, then drain well, allow them to become quite cold, and put them into jars. Boil the vinegar, spices, etc., together until sufficiently seasoned and flavoured, then pour the mixture, boiling hot, over the lemons, and cover closely. They will be ready for use in 6 months, and should in the meantime be kept in a cool, dry place.

LIMES, PICKLED (*See* Lemons, Pickled)

MANGO CHUTNEY, INDIAN

Procure 30 green mangoes, 2 lb. of sugar, ½ a lb. of salt, 2 lb. of raisins stoned, 1 lb. of green ginger, 3 oz. of dried chillies, 4 oz. of garlic and 3 pints of good vinegar.

Peel and slice the mangoes, chop them finely, also chop finely the raisins, green ginger and garlic. Pound the chillies in a mortar until smooth, then mix them with the rest of the prepared ingredients. Dissolve the sugar and salt in the vinegar, bring to the boil, then let it become quite cold and mix it with the mangoes, etc. Turn into wide-necked bottles or jars, cover closely, let them remain in the sun for 3 or 4 days, then store for use.

(See also recipe under Chutney, Mango.)

MANGO PICKLE, INDIAN

Have ready 50 green mangoes, 3 oz. of dried chillies, 1 lb. of green ginger finely sliced, ½ a lb. of mustard-seed, 2 oz. of garlic and 2 oz. of turmeric.

Peel the mangoes, and partly divide them through the shell, so as to remove the seed from the inside. Sprinkle them with salt, and let them remain for 24 hours. Meanwhile boil the turmeric in 2 quarts of vinegar for about 20 minutes, and let it become quite cold. Pound the chillies until smooth, add the ginger, the mustard-seed freed from husks, the garlic finely chopped, and mix well together. Fill the inside of the mangoes with this preparation, place them in jars, sprinkle over them any of the seasoning that remains, and cover with good malt vinegar.

MANGOES, PICKLED

Halve and stone the mangoes, stuff them with a mixture of sliced green ginger, mustard-seed and bruised garlic, replace the halves, and fasten them securely with strong cotton. Cover the mangoes with boiling spiced vinegar. On the following day strain off the vinegar, re-boil, and repeat the process on the two following days, four times in all. When cold, turn the preparation into jars, cover closely, and store in a dry, cool place.

MELON PICKLE

Cut the melon into quarters, peel thinly, and remove the seedy parts. Shred the pieces rather coarsely, and put them in a stone jar. Sprinkle with salt, and let them stand for 5 or 6 hours. Next pour over some wine vinegar diluted with water. To every pound of melon, weighed when drained, allow ½ lb. of sugar, 1 pint of vinegar, cinnamon stick, a little grated horseradish, some mustard-seeds, and a little ground olive to flavour. Cook these to the consistency of syrup, then add the drained melon. Pack in jars and cover them.

MELONS, PICKLED

Procure some small melons, small French beans, grated horseradish, cloves, ground nutmeg, cinnamon, pepper, vinegar, and to each quart add 1 teaspoonful each of cloves, allspice and black peppercorns.

Cut off one end, scoop out the inside of each melon, then replace and secure the end. Cover the melons with strong brine, let them remain undisturbed for 4 days, then drain and dry well. Sprinkle the inside of each melon liberally with cloves, cinnamon, nutmeg and pepper, and stuff them with well-seasoned French beans and horseradish. Replace, and tie on the ends, and pack the melons in a large jar, keeping the cut ends uppermost. Boil the vinegar and spices together for about 10 minutes, and, when cold, pour the liquid over the melons. On three consecutive days re-boil the vinegar, and pour it boiling over the melons. When cold, cover closely, and store in a cool, dry place.

MIXED PICKLES

To each gallon of vinegar allow ¼ of a lb. of bruised ginger, ¼ of a lb. of mustard, ¼ of a lb. of salt, 2 oz. of mustard-seed, 1 ½ oz. of turmeric, 1 oz. of ground black pepper, ¼ of an oz. of cayenne, cauliflowers, onions, celery, gherkins, French beans, nasturtiums, capsicums.

Have a large jar, with a tight-fitting lid, in which put as much vinegar as required, reserving a little to mix the various powders to a smooth paste. Put into a basin the mustard, turmeric, pepper and cayenne; mix them with vinegar, and stir well until no lumps remain; add all the ingredients to the vinegar, and mix well. Keep this liquor in a warm place, and thoroughly stir it every morning for 1 month with a wooden spoon, when it will be ready for the different vegetables to be added to it. As these come in season, have them gathered on a dry day, and after merely wiping them with a cloth, to free them from moisture, put them into the pickle. The cauliflowers must be divided into small bunches. Put all these into the pickle raw, and at the end of the season, when as many of the vegetables as could be procured have been added, store the pickle away in jars, and tie over with bladder. This old-fashioned method of preserving vegetables is largely employed by those who live in the country. The pickle should always be kept for at least 3 months in a cool, dry place before being used.

MIXED PICKLES II

Take an equal weight of small mild onions, sour apples and cucumbers, and sufficient vinegar to cover. To each pint of vinegar add 2 tablespoonfuls of sherry, 1 teaspoonful of salt, ½ a teaspoonful of pepper, a good pinch of cayenne.

Peel and slice the onions, apples and cucumbers thinly, put them into wide-necked bottles, add the seasoning and sherry, cover with vinegar, and cork closely. This pickle may be used the following day, and should not be kept for any length of time.

MIXED PICKLES III

Have at hand 1 lb. of onions, 1 lb. of apples, ¼ of a lb. of chillies, 1½ pints of white-wine vinegar and 1 good tablespoonful of salt.

Chop the onions and apples coarsely, and the chillies finely. Boil the vinegar, add the salt, and when dissolved pour over the prepared ingredients. Turn into small jars, and, when cold, cover closely.

MUSHROOMS, PICKLED

Wash, dry, and peel 1 quart of button mushrooms, and cut off the tops of the stalks. Place them in a stewpan, sprinkle salt to taste over them, shake them over the fire until the liquor flows, and keep them on the stove uncovered until the greater part of the moisture has evaporated. Then add 1 quart of vinegar, 1 oz. of bruised whole ginger, ½ oz. of white peppercorns and 3 blades of mace, bring to the boil, and simmer gently for about 10 minutes. Turn into jars, cover closely, and store in a cool, dry place.

Mushrooms

MUSHROOMS, PICKLED II

Take 1 quart of button mushrooms, 1 quart of vinegar, 1 oz. of whole ginger, ½ an oz. of white peppercorns and a good pinch of cayenne.

Cut off the tips of the stalks, rub off the outer skin with a piece of new flannel occasionally dipped in salt, rinse the mushrooms in salt and water, and dry them well. Boil the vinegar, pepper and spices together until pleasantly seasoned and flavoured, then put in the mushrooms and simmer them gently for about 10 minutes. Put into jars; when cold cover closely, and store in a cool, dry place until required for use.

NASTURTIUM SEEDS, PICKLED

Procure some nasturtium seeds and sufficient vinegar to cover them. To each pint of vinegar add ½ an oz. of salt and 6 peppercorns.

Boil the vinegar, salt and peppercorns together, and, when cold, strain it into a wide-necked bottle. Gather the seeds on a dry day, put them into the vinegar, and cork closely. These pickled seeds form an excellent substitute for capers. They are ready for use in about 3 months, but may be kept for a much longer time with perfect safety.

ONIONS, PICKLED

Have ready some pickling onions and sufficient vinegar to cover; to each quart of vinegar add 2 teaspoonfuls of allspice and 2 teaspoonfuls of whole black pepper.

Have the onions gathered when quite dry and ripe, and, with the fingers, take off the thin outside skin; then with a silver knife (steel should not be used, as it spoils the colour of the onions) remove one more skin, when the onions will look quite clear. Have ready some very dry bottles or jars, and as fast as the onions are peeled put them in. Pour over sufficient cold vinegar to cover them, with pepper and allspice in the above proportions, taking care that each jar has its share of the latter ingredients. Tie down with bladder, and put them in a dry place, and in a fortnight they will be ready for use.

Onions

ONIONS, PICKLED II

Take some silver onions and sufficient white wine vinegar to cover.

Remove the skins, throw the onions a few at a time into a saucepan of boiling water, taking care to have no more than will form a single layer floating on the surface of the water. As soon as the onions look clear on the outside take them up as quickly as possible with a slice, fold them in a clean dry cloth, so as to keep in the steam, and allow them to remain closely covered until the whole have been scalded. Let the onions be until quite cold, then put them into bottles or jars, and pour over them the vinegar, which should previously have been boiled and allowed to cool slightly. When cold, cover closely, and store in a cool, dry place.

PEACH PICKLE

Halve and stone 4 lb. of ripe peaches. Boil 2 quarts of pale brown vinegar with a dessertspoonful of whole pepper mixed, 2 red chillies cut up, a dessertspoonful each of coriander seeds and mustard-seeds, 2 inches of root ginger, ½ oz. of curry-powder, ½ lb. of brown sugar, and 2 to 3 oz. of salt. Add 2 or 3 onions, minced, and fried in oil to a light brown only, then put in the peaches as soon as the syrup boils up, and cook until quite done. Store in the usual manner.

PEACH PICKLE II

Have at hand 2 lb. of dried peaches, ½ a lb. of brown sugar, ½ a lb. of salt, 2 oz. of curry-powder, 6 large onions sliced, 6 chillies shredded, 6 large pieces of ginger, 1 tablespoonful of pepper, 1 tablespoonful of mustard-seeds, 1 tablespoonful of coriander seeds and 3 quarts of vinegar.

Pour the vinegar over the peaches and let them soak for at least 12 hours. Fry the sliced onions in salad-oil until well browned, and drain well. Pound or crush the spices. Boil all together until the peaches are quite soft but unbroken, then turn into jars or pots, cover closely, and store for use.

PEARS, SWEET, PICKLED

Select some nice firm pears. To each lb. allow ½ a lb. of brown sugar, and ¼ of a pint of malt vinegar, cloves, cinnamon, and allspice.

Peel the pears and tie the spices in muslin. Place the vinegar, sugar and spices in a preserving-pan; when boiling add the pears, and cook them gently until tender. Remove the pears to a bowl or large basin, boil the syrup for about 10 minutes longer, then pour it over the fruit. On the following day boil up the syrup, and repeat the process the two following days. On the third day place the pears in jars or wide-necked bottles, and remove the spices before adding the vinegar to the fruit. Store in a dry, cool place.

PICCALILLI

Procure some cauliflowers, onions, gherkins, French beans and capsicums.

Divide the vegetables into convenient pieces, throw them into boiling brine sufficiently strong to float an egg, and cook for 3 minutes. Drain well, spread them on large dishes, and

Capsicums

let them remain in the sun until perfectly dry. Prepare sufficient spiced vinegar and add ½ an oz. each of turmeric and curry-powder to each quart of vinegar. Also allow to each quart of vinegar 1 oz. of mustard, which must be mixed smoothly with a little cold vinegar, and afterwards stirred into the boiling vinegar, but not allowed to boil. Place the prepared vegetables in jars, cover them completely with vinegar, and when quite cold, cover closely.

PLUM PICKLE

The plums for this pickle may be red, purple or yellow, or mixed if more convenient; they must be ripe, but absolutely sound. Wipe them, prick them freely with a needle, and pack loosely into jars of about a quart capacity. Three-fourths fill them only with the fruit. Have ready the pickle made by boiling 3 level pints of granulated sugar with a quart of vinegar to a syrup, adding to this quantity 18 cloves, 3 inches of stick cinnamon, broken up, 12 black peppercorns, and a teaspoonful of allspice berries. These are to be bruised and left in the pickle. The jars must be filled, tied with bladder, and stored in a cool, dry place.

RADISH-PODS, PICKLED

Cover some young radish-pods with strong brine, let them remain for 12 hours, then drain the brine into a saucepan, and boil up. Pour the boiling brine over the pods, cover closely with a close-fitting lid or plate, let them remain undisturbed for 48 hours, then repeat the boiling process. Repeat again and again until the pods are perfectly green, then drain until they are quite dry, and pack them loosely in jars. Add 2 or 3 tablespoonfuls of grated horseradish to sufficient prepared and spiced vinegar, pour it boiling over the pods, and cover closely. On the following day strain, boil and replace the vinegar, and, when quite cold, tie down securely and store in a dry, cool place.

SHALLOT OR GARLIC PICKLE

To 2 quarts of the best white wine vinegar allow ½ a lb. of shallots or garlic, 2 oz. of whole ginger, 2 oz. of chillies, 4 oz. of mustard-seed and 2 oz. of turmeric.

Cover the ginger with strong brine made by boiling together 1 pint of water and 6 oz. of salt, let it remain for 5 days, then slice it thinly, and dry it in the sun. Peel the shallots or garlic, sprinkle liberally with salt, and let them remain thus for 3 days. Place the ginger, shallots, chillies, mustard-seed and turmeric in a wide-necked bottle, pour in the vinegar, cover closely, and store in a dry, cool place.

Garlic

SPANISH ONIONS, PICKLED

Peel some medium-sized onions, slice them thinly, place them in a large jar, and sprinkle each layer liberally with salt, and lightly with cayenne pepper. Cover the whole with vinegar, exclude the air by means of a bladder, or paper brushed over on both sides with white of egg, and store in a cool, dry place. The pickle will be ready for use in 10 or 14 days.

SWEET PICKLE

Take 7 lb. of peaches, pears or plums, 4 lb. of loaf or preserving sugar, 1 pint of good vinegar, 1 blade of mace, ½ an inch of cinnamon and 3 cloves.

Remove skins, stones or cores of the fruit, and place the fruit in a preserving-pan with alternate layers of sugar. Bring very slowly to boiling-point, then add the vinegar and spices, and boil for a few minutes. Take out the fruit with a skimmer, draining it well from the syrup, and place it on dishes to cool. Boil the syrup gently until thick, removing any scum as it rises, and pour it boiling over the fruit, which should be previously packed closely in glass jars. Cork tightly, and store in a cool, dry place. Examine frequently for the first month, and if there are any signs of fermentation, put the jars, uncovered, in a pan of water, and heat until they are scalding hot.

TOMATO CHOW CHOW

Have ready 6 large tomatoes, 1 Spanish onion, 1 green capsicum, 2 tablespoonfuls of brown sugar, 1 tablespoonful of salt, and ½ a pint of vinegar.

Peel and chop the onion coarsely. Blanch the tomatoes, remove the skins, and slice them finely. Place the onion and tomatoes in a stew-jar, add the capsicum finely chopped, the sugar, salt and vinegar, and cook in a slow oven until the onion is quite tender. When cold turn into small jars or wide-necked bottles, cover closely, and store in a cool, dry place.

TOMATO CHUTNEY (*See* recipe for Chutney, Tomato)

TOMATOES, PICKLED

Prepare some spiced vinegar, and to each quart add 1 dessertspoonful of moist sugar. Pack some small firm tomatoes loosely in a large jar, cover them with boiling vinegar, and put on a close-fitting lid or plate to keep in the steam. Tie down to exclude the air completely. This pickle will only keep for a short time.

TOMATOES AND ONIONS, PICKLED

Take an equal weight of firm tomatoes and medium-sized Spanish onions and sufficient good vinegar to cover. To each pint of vinegar allow 1 teaspoonful of peppercorns, ½ a teaspoonful of allspice and ½ a teaspoonful of salt.

Peel the onions, place them, with the tomatoes, compactly in a stewpan, add the salt, allspice and peppercorns tied together in muslin, cover with vinegar, and simmer very

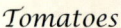

Tomatoes

gently for 5 or 6 hours. Turn into wide-necked bottles or jars; when cold cover closely and store in a cool, dry place until required.

VEGETABLE MARROWS, PICKLED

Procure some nice young vegetable marrows and sufficient vinegar to cover. To each quart of vinegar add 4 oz. of sugar, 1½ oz. of ginger broken into small pieces, 1¼ oz. of dry mustard, ½ an oz. of turmeric, 6 chillies and 1 clove of garlic finely chopped.

Boil the vinegar with the seasoning and flavouring ingredients until some of their strength and flavour is extracted. Meanwhile pare the marrows, cut them into 2-inch pieces, and remove the seeds. Add them to the boiling vinegar, cook gently for about 10 minutes, and turn into a large basin or earthenware pan. When quite cold lift the pieces of marrow carefully into wide-necked bottles or unglazed jars, pour in the vinegar, and cover closely. The pickle will be ready in 2 or 3 weeks, and should be kept in a cool, dry place until required.

WALNUTS, PICKLED

Procure some green walnuts and sufficient vinegar to cover them. To each quart of vinegar allow 1 oz. of peppercorns, 1 oz. of allspice and 1 teaspoonful of salt.

Prick the walnuts well with a steel fork or large darning needle, put them into an earthenware bowl or pan, and cover them with strong cold brine previously made by boiling the necessary quantity of water with the addition of 4 oz. of salt to each quart of water. Stir the walnuts two or three times daily for 6 days, then drain them and cover with fresh brine. Let them remain 3 days, then again drain them, spread them on large dishes, and place them in the sun until quite black. Have ready some wide-necked bottles or unglazed jars, and three-quarters fill these with walnuts. Boil sufficient vinegar to cover them, with peppercorns, allspice and salt as stated above, for about 15 minutes, and when quite cold pour the mixture over the walnuts. If closely covered, and stored in a dry, cool place, they may be kept for months.

WALNUTS, PICKLED II

Have ready some green walnuts and sufficient vinegar to cover them. To 3 pints of vinegar allow 1 oz. of salt and ½ an oz. each of allspice, peppercorns, cloves and whole ginger.

Wipe the walnuts with a dry cloth, put them into wide-necked bottles, or unglazed jars, and cover them with cold vinegar. Cover closely, let them stand in a cool, dry place for 4 months, then drain off the vinegar. Boil as much fresh vinegar as will cover them, with the seasonings as stated above, and pour it, while boiling hot, over the walnuts. Cover closely, and store for 3 weeks in a cool, dry place, the walnuts will then be ready for use.

Walnuts

Still Life by Estêvão Silva (1888)

CHAPTER XI

MISCELLANEOUS PRESERVES AND PICKLES

COCKLES, PICKLED

The large cockles found on the north-east coast are the best for this purpose. Wash them in several waters to remove the grit; when quite free from it cover the cockles with cold water, add a good handful each of salt and oatmeal, and let them remain until the following day. To each quart of cockles allow a small ½ teaspoonful of allspice, and the same quantity of peppercorns. Tie these spices in muslin and boil them for about 20 minutes in sufficient vinegar to cover the cockles. Put the cockles into a steamer, or, failing this, a large iron saucepan with 2 or 3 tablespoonfuls of water to protect the bottom of the pan, cover them: first with a wet kitchen-cloth, then the lid, and cook the cockles slowly until their shells may be easily opened with the point of a knife (about 15 minutes). Put the cockles into the prepared cold vinegar, and the liquor contained in the shells into a basin, and as soon as it is cold strain it into the vinegar. Cockles or oysters pickled in this way may be kept some days.

CUCUMBERS, PRESERVED

Pare and slice the cucumbers thinly, sprinkle liberally with salt, and let them remain until the following day. Drain off the liquor, pack the slices closely in jars, sprinkling each layer thickly with salt, and cover with parchment paper, or paper coated on both sides with white of egg. When wanted for use, wash well in cold water, drain well, and dress with pepper, vinegar and oil.

EGGS, PICKLED

Take 16 hard-boiled eggs, 1 quart of good vinegar, ½ an oz. of black peppercorns, ½ an oz. of allspice, and ½ an oz. of ginger.

Remove the shells, and arrange the eggs compactly in wide-necked jars. Boil the peppercorns, spice and ginger in the vinegar until some of their flavour is extracted, and pour it whilst boiling hot over the eggs. When cold, cover closely, and store in a cool, dry place.

Mushrooms

MUSHROOMS, BOTTLED

Procure about 2 lb. of small button mushrooms and wipe them with a clean, dry cloth. Peel carefully, and trim off the stalks. Put the mushrooms into a basin and sprinkle with salt. Pour some well-diluted wine vinegar over the mushrooms and bring slowly to the boil. Shake them well, pour off the liquid and drain them. Then boil the mushrooms again, using a fresh lot of diluted vinegar. Remove the pan from the fire as soon as boiling and bottle the mushrooms as soon as they are cool, with enough vinegar to well cover. Cork and seal the bottles, wrap them round with straw and steam or boil from 2 to 3 hours according to size.

Large mushrooms may be treated in exactly the same manner, but the red portion of the stalks should be removed. Mushrooms which are black round the stalks are unsuitable for preserving.

MUSHROOMS, TO KEEP TEMPORARILY

Peel, wash, and thoroughly dry 1 quart of mushrooms.

Heat 2 oz. of butter in a LARGE stewpan, put in the mushrooms, season lightly with salt and pepper, and add 1 tablespoonful of lemon-juice. Leave the pan uncovered, and cook the mushrooms very slowly, until they become quite dry. They will keep good for several days, and when required for use should be reheated and drained free from butter. They may also be kept for some time if closely packed in a shallow pie-dish, and covered with clarified butter.

MUSHROOMS, TO PRESERVE

To each quart of mushrooms allow 3 oz. of butter, pepper and salt to taste, the juice of 1 lemon and clarified butter.

Peel the mushrooms, put them into cold water, with a little lemon-juice; let them remain for about 10 minutes, then dry them very carefully in a cloth. Put the butter into a stewpan capable of holding the mushrooms; when it is melted, add the mushrooms, lemon-juice, and a seasoning of pepper and salt. Draw them down over a slow fire, and let them remain until their liquor is boiled away, and they have become quite dry, but they must not stick to the bottom of the stewpan. When done, put the mushrooms into pots, and over the top pour clarified butter. If not wanted for immediate use, they will keep good a few days without being covered over. To re-warm them, put the mushrooms into a stewpan, strain the butter from them, and they will be ready for use.

OYSTERS, PICKLED

Blanch the oysters in their own liquor, but in other details follow directions for Cockles, Pickled.

TOMATO CONSERVE

Procure 3 lb. of nice ripe tomatoes, ½ a pint of vinegar, 1 dessertspoonful of castor sugar, 1 teaspoonful of ground ginger, $\frac{1}{8}$ of an oz. of garlic, ½ a teaspoonful of allspice, and 1 dessertspoonful of salt.

Bake the tomatoes in the oven until quite tender, then skin and place them in a stone jar with the above-mentioned flavouring ingredients. Mix all together thoroughly and keep in a cool place for a few days. Then rub the tomato pulp through a fine sieve and boil up in an earthenware pan with a little more vinegar than sugar. Bottle when cool, cork and seal the bottles and store them away in a cool, dry place until required for use.

Capsicums, shallots and lemon-juice may be added if liked, but the conserve then becomes more of a condiment than a simple tomato conserve with its own natural flavour.

VEGETABLES, TO PRESERVE

Nearly every kind of vegetable may be preserved by steaming in salt water and then filling into jars. It must be remembered that vegetables take longer to cook than fruit. After corking the bottles stand them upside down to see if they leak.

Miscellaneous Preserves and Pickles

Stillleben mit Austern und Zitrone [Still Life with Oysters and Lemon] by Peter Jacob Horemans (1769)

CHAPTER XII

STORE OR CONDIMENT SAUCES

ANCHOVIES, ESSENCE OF

Take 1 lb. of anchovies, 1 pint of cold water, ¼ of a pint of good vinegar, 1 saltspoonful of ground mace, and 1 saltspoonful of cayenne.

Pound the anchovies in a mortar until smooth, and pass them through a fine sieve. Put the parts that will not pass through the sieve into a stewpan, add any liquor there may be in the bottles from which the anchovies were taken, the mace, cayenne, and water, simmer gently for about ½ an hour, then strain, and mix it with the anchovy puree. Return the mixture to the stewpan, bring to boiling-point, add the vinegar, simmer very gently for about 10 minutes longer, and when quite cold pour into small bottles. Cork securely, cover the corks with melted wax, and store for use in a cool, dry place.

ANCHOVY KETCHUP

Put 1 quart of good ale, ¼ of a lb. of anchovies, 3 finely-chopped shallots, 3 tablespoonfuls of mushroom ketchup, ½ a teaspoonful of castor sugar, ½ a teaspoonful of ground ginger, ¼ of a teaspoonful of ground mace, and 2 cloves into a stewpan, simmer very gently for about 1 hour, and strain. When quite cold, pour the ketchup into small bottles, cork them tightly, and store in a cool, dry place.

BENTON SAUCE (For Hot or Cold Roast Beef)

Mix 4 tablespoonfuls of vinegar, 1 tablespoonful of scraped horseradish, 1 teaspoonful of made mustard, and 1 teaspoonful of castor sugar well together, and serve.

BOAR'S HEAD SAUCE (For Game or Cold Meat)

Take ½ a pint of dissolved red-currant jelly, a small glass of port wine, 4 oranges, 1 oz. of sugar, 1 finely-chopped shallot, 1 mustardspoonful of mixed mustard and a seasoning of pepper.

Shred the rind of 2 oranges into very fine strips, and rub the lumps of sugar over the rinds of the remaining two. Put the rind and sugar into the liquid jelly, add the wine, shallot,

Anchovy

mustard, and a liberal seasoning of pepper, and use as required, or the sauce may be put into well-corked bottles and stored for use.

CAMBRIDGE SAUCE (For Roast Duck, Cold Meat, etc.)

Have ready 2 tablespoonfuls of olive oil, 3 tablespoonfuls of tarragon vinegar, 4 hard-boiled yolks of eggs, 4 fillets of anchovies, 1 tablespoonful of capers, 1 dessertspoonful of French mustard, 1 teaspoonful of English mustard, 1 teaspoonful of finely-chopped parsley, a sprig of tarragon, a sprig of chervil and a pinch of cayenne.

Pound all the ingredients except the parsley well together, then pass through a hair sieve. If too stiff, add a little oil and vinegar gradually until the consistency resembles that of mayonnaise sauce. Stir in the parsley and keep on ice until required.

CAMP VINEGAR

Take 1 head of garlic, ½ an oz. of cayenne, 2 teaspoonfuls of soy, 2 tablespoonfuls of walnut ketchup, 1 pint of vinegar, and sufficient cochineal to colour.

Slice the garlic, and put it, with all the above ingredients, into a clean bottle. Let it stand to infuse for 1 month, then strain it off quite clear, and it will be fit for use. Keep it in small bottles, well sealed to exclude the air.

CARRACK SAUCE (For Cold Meat)

Mix 1 quart of vinegar, 5 dessertspoonfuls of mushroom ketchup, 5 dessertspoonfuls of soy, 8 dessertspoonfuls of coarsely-chopped pickled walnuts, 3 dessertspoonfuls of coarsely-chopped mango pickle, ½ an oz. of garlic bruised, and 15 anchovies finely chopped well together in a bottle, let it remain in a warm place, and shake it daily for a month, when it will be ready.

CAYENNE VINEGAR

Mix 2 quarts of vinegar and 1½ oz. of cayenne pepper together in a bottle, let it stand for 1 month, shaking the preparation daily. When ready, strain into clean, dry bottles, cork them, and store for use.

CELERY VINEGAR

Have at hand ½ a lb. of finely-shredded celery, or ½ an oz. of celery seed, 1 pint of good pickling vinegar, and 1 level teaspoonful of salt.

Boil the vinegar, dissolve the salt in it, and pour the mixture over the celery or celery seed. When cold, cover and let it remain undisturbed for 3 weeks, strain into small bottles, and cork securely.

CHEROKEE

Put 1 quart of best malt vinegar, ½ a pint of walnut ketchup, 4 tablespoonfuls of soy, 1 oz. of cayenne, and 3 minced cloves of garlic into a large bottle, cork tightly, and let them remain undisturbed for 1 month. At the end of this time, strain the liquid into small bottles, cork securely and store.

CHILLI VINEGAR

Procure 50 fresh chillies and 1 pint of good pickling vinegar. Cut the chillies in halves. Boil the vinegar, let it become quite cold, then pour it over the chillies. Cork closely, and store.

CRESS VINEGAR

Take ½ an oz. of cress seed and 1 quart of vinegar.

Bruise the seed in a mortar, and put it into the vinegar, previously boiled and allowed to grow cold. Let it infuse for a fortnight, then strain and bottle for use.

CUCUMBER KETCHUP

Peel the cucumbers, slice them as thinly as possible into a basin, and sprinkle them liberally with salt. Let them remain closely covered until the following day, then strain the liquor from the cucumbers into a stewpan, add 1 teaspoonful of peppercorns to each pint, and simmer gently for about ½ an hour. When cold, strain into bottles, cork tightly, and store in a cool, dry place. This ketchup imparts an agreeable flavour to sweetbreads, calf's brains, chicken mixtures, and other delicate preparations.

CUCUMBER VINEGAR

Have ready 6 cucumbers and 1 quart of vinegar. To each pint of vinegar allow 2 shallots, 1 clove of garlic, 1 teaspoonful of white peppercorns, and 1 teaspoonful of salt.

Boil the vinegar, salt and peppercorns together for about 20 minutes, and allow the mixture to become quite cold. Slice the cucumbers without paring them into a wide-necked bottle or jar, add the shallots and garlic, and the vinegar when cold. Let the preparation remain closely covered for fourteen days, then carefully strain off into smaller bottles, cork tightly, and store in a cool, dry place.

ESCAVEEKE SAUCE

Procure 1 quart of French white wine vinegar, the finely-grated rinds of 2 lemons, 12 shallots, 4 cloves of garlic, 2 tablespoonfuls of coriander seed, 1 teaspoonful of ground ginger, 1 teaspoonful of salt, and 1 level teaspoonful of cayenne.

Cucumber

Pound all the dry ingredients well together, and put them into an earthenware vessel. Boil the vinegar, and add it, boiling hot, to the pounded preparation. When quite cold, pour into small bottles, cork tightly, and store for use. It is important to keep this sauce in a cool and dry place, otherwise it will not keep.

FISH CONDIMENT SAUCE

Put 1 quart of malt vinegar, 2 tablespoonfuls of walnut ketchup, 2 tablespoonfuls of soy, 1 oz. of cayenne, 1 clove of garlic, and 2 shallots sliced into a large bottle, and shake them daily for a fortnight. When ready, strain into small bottles, cork securely, and store for use.

GARLIC VINEGAR (*See* Shallot Vinegar)

Use Garlic in place of Shallots.

HARVEY SAUCE (For Cold Meat and Salads)

Take 1 quart of good vinegar, 3 anchovies, 1 tablespoonful of soy, 1 gill of walnut ketchup, 1 finely-chopped shallot, 1 finely-chopped clove of garlic, ¼ of an oz. of cayenne and a few drops of cochineal to improve the colour.

Cut each anchovy into 3 or 4 pieces, place them in a wide-necked bottle or unglazed jar, add the shallots, garlic and the rest of the ingredients, and cover closely. Let the jar stand for 14 days, during which time the contents must be either shaken or stirred at least once a day. At the end of this time strain into small bottles, cork them securely, and store the sauce in a cool, dry place until required.

HERB SAUCE (For Flavouring Gravies and Stews)

Take 1 stick of horseradish, 2 finely-chopped shallots, a few sprigs each of winter savory, basil, marjoram, thyme, tarragon, 6 cloves, the thinly-peeled rind and juice of 1 lemon, ½ a pint of strong vinegar and 1 pint of water.

Wash and scrape the horseradish; and remove the stalks of the herbs. Put all the ingredients together in a stewpan, simmer gently for about 20 minutes, then strain, and, when quite cold, pour into small bottles. Cork securely and store for use.

HORSERADISH VINEGAR

Have ready 8 oz. of grated horseradish, 1 tablespoonful of finely-chopped shallots, 1 heaped teaspoonful of salt, ½ a teaspoonful of cayenne, and 4 pints of good malt vinegar.

Mix the horseradish, shallots, salt and cayenne together, boil the vinegar and pour it over them, cover closely, and allow the vessel to stand in a warm, but not hot, place for 10 days.

Thyme

Strain the vinegar into a stewpan, bring to boiling point, let it cool, then pour into small bottles, cork closely, and store in a cool, dry place.

INDIAN MUSTARD

Take ¼ of a lb. of mustard, ¼ of a lb. of flour, ½ an oz. of salt, 4 shallots chopped, 1 gill of vinegar, 4 tablespoonfuls of mushroom ketchup, and 2 tablespoonfuls of anchovy sauce.

Put the mustard, flour and salt into a basin, and mix them into a smooth paste with hot water. Boil the shallots with the vinegar, ketchup and anchovy sauce for about 10 minutes, then add the blended flour, etc., and stir and simmer gently for 2 or 3 minutes. When quite cold pour the preparation into small bottles, cork them tightly, and store in a cool, dry place.

KETCHUP (*See* Mushroom Ketchup, etc.)

KETCHUP, PONTAC

Procure 1 quart of ripe elderberries, ½ a lb. of anchovies, 6 shallots, 1 pint of vinegar, 6 cloves, 2 blades of mace, and about 24 peppercorns.

Remove the stalks, place the berries in a jar, cover them with vinegar, cook in a moderately hot oven for 3 hours, then strain and measure the vinegar. To each quart add ½ a lb. of coarsely-chopped anchovies, 1 oz. of chopped shallots, 6 cloves, 2 blades of mace, and 24 peppercorns. Simmer gently for about 1 hour, then strain and bottle for use.

LEAMINGTON SAUCE (For Cold Meat and Fish)

Procure young green walnuts, pound them to a pulp, sprinkle liberally with salt, and let them remain for 3 days, stirring at frequent intervals. Strain the juice obtained, measure and for each pint of walnut juice add 3 pints of vinegar, ½ a pint of Indian soy, ¼ of a pint of port wine, 1 oz. of shallots, ¼ of an oz. of garlic and ½ an oz. of cayenne, the garlic and shallots being previously pounded or finely chopped. Turn the whole into a large jar, cover closely for 3 weeks, then strain into small bottles, cork and seal securely, and store for use.

Elderberries

MINT VINEGAR

The mint for this purpose must be young and fresh. Pick the leaves from the stalks, and fill a bottle or jar with them. Cover with cold vinegar, cover closely, and let the mint infuse for 14 days. Then strain the liquor into small bottles, cork securely, and store for use.

Store or Condiment Sauces

MUSHROOM KETCHUP

Mushrooms intended for this purpose should be gathered on a dry day, otherwise the ketchup will not keep. Trim the tips of the stalks, but do not wash nor peel the mushrooms; simply rub any part not quite clean with a little salt. Place them in a large jar, sprinkling each layer liberally with salt. Let them remain for 3 days, stirring them at least 3 times daily. At the end of that time, cook them very gently either on the stove or in a cool oven, until the juice flows freely, then strain the mushrooms through a clean cloth, and drain well, but do not squeeze them.

Replace the liquor in the jar; to 1 quart of mushroom liquor add ½ an oz. of allspice, ½ an oz. of ground ginger, ¼ of a teaspoonful of pounded mace, and ¼ of a teaspoonful of cayenne, place the jar in a saucepan of boiling water, and cook very gently for 3 hours. Strain 2 or 3 times through fine muslin when quite cold, pour into small bottles, cork securely, and store for use.

HOW TO DISTINGUISH MUSHROOMS FROM TOADSTOOLS

The cultivated mushroom, known as **Agaricus campestris**, may be distinguished from the poisonous kinds of fungi by its having pink or flesh-coloured gills, or under side, and by its having invariably an agreeable smell, which the toadstool has not. When young, mushrooms are like a small round button, both the stalk and head being white. As they grow larger they expand their heads by degrees into a flat form, the gills underneath being first of a pale flesh colour, but becoming, as they stand longer, dark brown or blackish. Nearly all the poisonous kinds are brown, and have in general a rank and putrid smell. Edible mushrooms are found in closely fed pastures, but seldom grow in woods, where most of the poisonous sorts flourish. [We would advise great caution when picking and eating wild mushrooms. If in doubt, consult an expert or a reputable guide to mushrooms and toadstools.]

MUSTAPHA, OR LIVER KETCHUP

Take 1 ox-liver, 1 gallon of water, 1 oz. of ginger, 1 oz. of allspice, 2 oz. of whole black pepper, and 2 lb. of salt.

Rub the salt well into a very fresh ox-liver, and place it in a vessel without crushing. Turn and rub it thoroughly daily for 10 days. Mince it up rather small, and boil in a gallon of water, closely covered until reduced to 3 quarts. Strain through a sieve, put it aside until the following day, then add the pepper, allspice, and ginger, and boil slowly until reduced to 2 quarts. When cold, bottle and keep well corked. [We recommend that, if you are brave

Ox

enough to make this ketchup, the ox-liver and the ketchup should be kept in the fridge and only stored for a very short period.]

PIQUANT SAUCE (As Condiment)

Procure 100 green walnuts, 5 lb. of fresh mushrooms, and sufficient vinegar to cover. To each pint of vinegar allow 1 teaspoonful of soy, 6 shallots, 1 clove of garlic, ½ a teaspoonful of ground ginger, ½ a teaspoonful of mustard-seed, ¼ of a teaspoonful of allspice, 2 cloves, 1 blade of mace, and ¼ of a saltspoonful of cayenne.

Place the mushrooms and walnuts in separate earthenware bowls or pans, bruise them well with a pestle or wooden potato-masher, or, failing these, a heavy wooden spoon, and sprinkle them lightly with salt. Let them lie for a week. Turn and bruise them daily, then drain off the liquor, and squeeze the pulp as dry as possible. As a rule the quantity of juice thus obtained from the walnuts and mushrooms is nearly equal. Mix the two together, and boil gently until the scum, which must be carefully removed, ceases to rise. Measure the liquid, return it to the pan with an equal quantity of vinegar, and shallots, garlic, ginger, mustard-seed, allspice, cloves, mace, and cayenne in the above-stated proportions. Simmer gently for about ½ an hour, skimming well meanwhile, then turn the liquid into an earthenware vessel, and add the soy. When quite cold, pour the sauce into small bottles, cork closely, and store in a dry, cool place until required for use.

QUIN'S SAUCE (For Roast Duck, Turkey, Pork, etc.)

Put 1 pint of mushroom ketchup, ½ a pint of walnut pickle, ½ a pint of port wine, ¼ of a pint of soy, 12 anchovies chopped, 12 shallots chopped, and ½ a teaspoonful of cayenne into a saucepan, simmer gently for about 15 minutes, and strain. When quite cold, bottle, cork and seal securely, and store for use.

RASPBERRY VINEGAR

Take 3 to 4 lb. of raspberries, 3 to 4 pints of vinegar, and sugar to taste.

Cover the raspberries with vinegar, let them remain undisturbed for 4 days, then strain through a fine hair sieve, but do not press the fruit. Pour the vinegar over a fresh lot of raspberries and proceed as before. Repeat this process two or three times, taking care to drain each lot thoroughly. Measure the vinegar, to each pint add 4 to 5 oz. of sugar, simmer gently for 10 minutes, skimming well meanwhile. When quite cold, bottle for use. Or, put equal measures of raspberries and vinegar into a large jar, stir the mixture two or three times daily for 10 days, then strain off the vinegar. Measure it, adding about 2 oz. of sugar to each pint, boil up, skim well, and, when cold, bottle for use.

Raspberries

Shallots

READING SAUCE (For Cold Meat, etc.)

Take 1 quart of walnut pickle, 1 quart of cold water, ½ a pint of soy, 1½ oz. of shallots, ½ an oz. of whole ginger bruised, ½ an oz. of capsicums, 1 oz. of mustard-seed, ½ an oz. of cayenne, ¼ of an oz. of bay-leaves, and 1 tablespoonful essence of anchovy.

Peel the shallots, chop them finely, place them in a fireproof jar with the liquor strained from the walnuts, and simmer gently until considerably reduced. In another fireproof jar put the water, soy, ginger, capsicums, mustard-seed, cayenne, and essence of anchovy, bring to the boil, and simmer gently for about 1 hour. Now mix the contents of the two jars together, and continue the slow cooking for about ½ an hour longer. Let the jar remain closely covered in a cool place until the following day, then add the bay-leaves, re-place the cover, and allow the jar to remain undisturbed for 7 days. At the end of this time, strain off the liquor into small bottles, and store for use.

SAUCE FOR STEAKS, CHOPS, ETC.

Have at hand 1 pint of mushroom ketchup or walnut pickle, ½ an oz. of pickled shallots, ½ an oz. of grated horseradish, ½ an oz. of allspice, 1 oz. of black pepper, and 1 oz. of salt.

Pound the shallots and horseradish until smooth in a mortar, add the rest of the ingredients, and let the whole stand closely covered for 14 days. Strain into small bottles, cork and seal securely, and store for use.

SHALLOT SAUCE (As Condiment)

Procure 1 pint of sherry, 1 pint of vinegar and 4 oz. of shallots.

Skin the shallots, chop them finely, and put them into a wide-necked bottle. Pour over them the sherry and the vinegar, let them remain closely corked for 14 days, then strain off the liquor into small bottles. Cork lightly, and store for use.

SHALLOT VINEGAR

Allow 1 quart of good vinegar to 4 oz. of shallots. Remove the skins, chop the shallots finely, and put them into a wide-necked bottle. Pour in the vinegar, cork securely, and put the bottle aside for 10 days, during which time it must be shaken at least once a day. At the end of this time strain the vinegar through fine muslin, put it into small bottles, cork closely, and store for use.

SOY, INDIAN

This sauce is usually bought ready prepared. It is imported from China and Japan, where it is made from a small bean, the produce of Dolichos Soja. Japanese soy is usually preferred to that of China, because it is free from the sweet treacly flavour which distinguishes the latter. When well made it has a good brown colour, thick consistence, and is clear.

STORE SAUCE (For Cold Meat, etc.)

Procure 1 pint of mushroom ketchup, ½ a pint of walnut ketchup, ¼ of a pint of port wine, 12 anchovies, 6 shallots, and 2 tablespoonfuls of cayenne.

Pound the anchovies and shallots, or chop them finely; add them to the rest of the ingredients, and boil gently for about 1 hour. When cold, put the preparation into well-corked bottles, and store for use.

TAMARIND SAUCE (For Fruit Salads or Cold Meat)

Place ripe tamarinds in layers in a stone jar, sprinkling each layer slightly or liberally with sugar, according to taste. Cook in a cool oven until quite tender, then pass through a fine hair sieve, and when quite cold pour into small bottles, cork and seal securely, and store for use.

TARRAGON VINEGAR

Tarragon leaves intended for this purpose should be gathered on a dry day about the end of July, just before the plant begins to bloom. Remove the stalks, bruise the leaves slightly, put them into a wide-necked bottle, and cover them with vinegar. Cover closely so as to completely exclude the air, and let the bottle stand in a cool, dry place for 7 or 8 weeks. Now strain the liquid through fine muslin until it is quite clear, put it into small bottles, cork tightly, and store them in a cool, dry place.

Tamarind

TOMATO KETCHUP

Take 2 lb. of ripe tomatoes, 2 onions, 4 green pepper-pods, 2 tablespoonfuls of salt, 2 teaspoonfuls of moist sugar (Demerara), 1 tablespoonful of ground ginger, ½ a teaspoonful of mustard, 1 ground nutmeg, and 2 quarts of vinegar.

Peel and crush the tomatoes, and peel and slice the onions; chop the green pepper-pods finely. Put these with all the other ingredients, carefully mixed, in a stewpan, and boil for about 2 hours, stirring frequently. Rub all through a sieve, bottle whilst hot, and store in a cool, dry place.

TOMATO SAUCE

Bake the tomatoes in a slow oven until tender, rub them through a fine sieve, and measure the pulp. To each quart of tomato pulp allow 1 pint of chilli vinegar, ¼ of a pint of soy,

1 tablespoonful of anchovy-essence, 2 finely-chopped shallots, 1 finely-chopped clove of garlic and salt to taste. Put the pulp into a stewpan, add the rest of the ingredients, simmer until the shallots and garlic are quite tender, and pass the whole through a tammy or fine hair sieve. Store in air-tight bottles.

TOMATO SAUCE II

Take 12 large tomatoes, 2 Spanish onions, 1 oz. of salt, ½ a teaspoonful of cayenne, and 1 pint of vinegar.

Peel the onions, slice them thinly, place them in a stewjar with the tomatoes, and cook in a slow oven until tender. Pass the pulp through a fine hair sieve, put it into a stewpan with the vinegar, salt and cayenne, and simmer gently for about 10 minutes. Store for use in small air-tight bottles.

TOMATO VINEGAR

Have at hand 18 sound tomatoes, 3 or 4 oz. of salt, 1 quart of good vinegar, ¼ of a pint of mustard-seed, mace, cloves and nutmeg.

Cut each tomato across into quarters, but without separating them at the bottom. Place them in a large jar, sprinkling each layer with salt, and cook them in a very slow oven for 12 hours. Add the mustard-seed and spices to taste, boil and add the vinegar, and cover closely. Let the jar stand by the side of the stove for 5 or 6 days, and either stir or shake it several times daily. When ready strain into small bottles, cork them securely, and store for use.

VINEGAR, SPICED

Take 1 quart of good vinegar, 2 oz. of black peppercorns, 1 oz. of whole ginger, ½ an oz. of salt, ½ an oz. of allspice, 1 oz. of finely-chopped shallots, 2 cloves of garlic bruised and 2 bay-leaves.

Pound or crush the peppercorns, ginger and allspice, put all into a jar, add the rest of the ingredients, and cover closely. Let the jar remain in a warm place for 1 week, then place it in a saucepan containing boiling water, and cook gently for about 1 hour. When cold, cover closely, and store for use.

WALNUT KETCHUP

Procure 100 green walnuts, 2 quarts of good vinegar, 3 oz. of salt, 4 oz. of anchovies, 12 finely-chopped shallots, ½ a stick of finely-grated horseradish, ½ a teaspoonful each of mace, nutmeg, ground ginger, ground cloves and pepper and ½ a pint of port.

Bay Leaves

The walnuts must be very young and tender. Bruise them slightly, put them into a jar with the salt and vinegar, and let them remain for 8 days, stirring them daily. Drain the liquor from them into a stewpan, add to it the rest of the ingredients, simmer very gently for about 40 minutes, and when quite cold, strain the preparation into small bottles. Cork them closely, cover the corks with melted wax, and store in a cool, dry place.

WORCESTER SAUCE (For Cold Meat or Fish)

Put 1 quart of best brown vinegar, 6 tablespoonfuls of walnut ketchup, 5 tablespoonfuls of essence of anchovy, 4 tablespoonfuls of soy, ½ a teaspoonful of cayenne, 4 very finely-chopped shallots, and salt to taste into a large bottle, and cork it closely. Shake it well three or four times daily for about 14 days, then strain the sauce into small bottles, cork them tightly, and store in a cool, dry place.

Walnuts

Still Life on Kitchen Table with Celery, Parsley, Bowl, and Cruets by Léon Bonvin (1865)

CHAPTER XIII

HOME-MADE WINES AND FRUIT SYRUPS

APPLE WINE

Put 5 gallons of good cider into a cask it will about three-quarters fill, add 10 lb. of loaf sugar, and stir occasionally with a piece of wood or cane until the sugar is quite dissolved; at the end of 48 hours put in the bung, and place a small vent-peg near the top of the cask. Allow the cask to remain for 12 months in a cool, dry place, when the wine will be ready for use.

APRICOT WINE

Take 12 lb. of sound but not over-ripe apricots, 1 lb. of loaf sugar, 1 pint of white wine, 3 gallons of water, 1 tablespoonful of compressed yeast, or 1 tablespoonful of good brewers' yeast.

Remove the stones of the fruit, take out the kernels, and cut each apricot into 6 or 8 pieces. Put them into a preserving-pan with the water, sugar, and about half the kernels, and simmer very gently for about 1 hour. Turn the whole into an earthenware vessel, let it remain undisturbed until cool, then stir in the yeast; if compressed yeast is used it must previously be mixed smoothly with a little warm water. Cover the vessel with a cloth, let it remain undisturbed for 3 days, then strain the liquid into a clean, dry cask, add the white wine, and bung lightly. At the end of 6 months draw off the wine into bottles, cork them closely, store in a cool, dry place for about 12 months, and the wine will then be ready for use.

BLACKBERRY SYRUP

To each lb. of fruit allow 1 lb. of loaf or preserving sugar and 1 tablespoonful of cold water.

Place the fruit, sugar and water in a large jar with a close-fitting cover, stand the jar in a saucepan of boiling water, and cook gently for about 2 hours. Strain the juice, measure it, put it into a preserving-pan or stewpan (preferably an enamelled one), and boil gently for about 20 minutes, skimming carefully meanwhile. To each pint of syrup add a small glass of brandy, let it become quite cold, then bottle for use.

CHERRY BOUNCE

Remove the stones, place the fruit in a large jar, and stand the jar in a saucepan containing boiling water. Cook gently until all the juice is extracted, strain it, and measure it into a preserving-pan. To each gallon of juice add 4 lb. of sugar, ½ a teaspoonful of ground mace, ¼ of a teaspoonful of ground allspice, 1 quart of brandy, and 1 quart of rum, and simmer the ingredients until the scum ceases to rise. When cold, add the spirits, and bottle for use.

CHERRY WINE

Place the cherries, preferably small black ones, on a large dish and bruise them well with a large wooden spoon. Allow them to remain until the following day, then drain them well on a hair sieve, and measure the juice into an earthenware vessel. To each quart of juice add ½ lb. of loaf or good preserving sugar, cover the vessel, let it stand for 24 hours, and strain the liquor into a clean, dry cask. Bung closely, but provide the upper part of the cask with a vent-peg; let it remain undisturbed for about 6 months, then drain off into bottles. Cork closely, and store in a cool, dry place.

CHERRY WINE II

Stone the cherries, which should be nice and ripe, put them into a large jar, place in a saucepan of boiling water, and cook gently until the juice is all extracted. Then strain and measure the juice into a preserving-pan. To each quart of juice allow a pinch each of ground mace, ground cloves and ground allspice, ½ a pint of brandy and ½ a pint of rum. Add sugar and the above ingredients, and boil and skim until clear. Let it cool, add the spirits, pour into bottles, and cork them closely.

CIDER

The method of making cider varies according to localities. It is a product, i.e. the juice of the apple (sour or tart kinds for preference). The apples should not be collected until sufficiently matured, and the fruit should be left from 14 to 16 days in a barn or loft to mellow. During that time the mucilage decomposes and the alcohol and carbonic acid are being developed. The juice is next extracted, and this is usually done by pulping or grinding the apples by means of a mill which consists of two cylinders of hard wood or cast-iron or steel working against one another. The pulp so obtained is pressed with heavy weights so

Cider apple

as to extract all the juice, which is then placed in a large tub and kept at a heat of about 60°. After allowing it to stand for about a week the sediment will have subsided, and the clear liquor can be drawn off into casks. These are then stored in a cellar or other cool place, but must be kept at a regular or even temperature.

CLARY WINE

To each gallon of water allow 3 lb. of either loaf or good preserving sugar, 2 tablespoonfuls of brewers' yeast, or ¼ of an oz. of compressed yeast moistened with water, 1 quart of clary flowers and tops and ½ a pint of good brandy.

Dissolve the sugar in the water, bring to the boil, simmer gently for about 10 minutes, skimming meanwhile, and when cool pour it into a clean dry cask. Add a little of the warm syrup to the yeast, and when it is working well stir it, together with the clary flowers and tops, into the rest of the syrup. Stir vigorously twice daily for 5 days, and bung closely as soon as fermentation ceases. Let it remain undisturbed for 4 months, then drain it carefully from the sediment; add the brandy, pour into bottles, and cork securely. After being stored for about 6 months in a cool, dry place, it will be ready for use.

COWSLIP WINE

Procure 4 quarts of cowslip flowers, 4 quarts of water, 3 lb. of loaf sugar, the finely-grated rind and juice of 1 orange and 1 lemon, 2 tablespoonfuls of brewers' yeast, or ¼ of an oz. of compressed yeast moistened with water and ¼ of a pint of brandy, if liked.

Boil the sugar and water together for about ½ an hour, skimming when necessary, and pour, quite boiling, over the rinds and strained juice of the orange and lemon. Let it cool, then stir in the yeast and cowslip flowers, cover with a cloth, and allow it to remain undisturbed for 48 hours. Turn the whole into a clean dry cask, add the brandy, bung closely, let it remain thus for 8 weeks, then draw it off into bottles. Cork securely, store in a cool, dry place for 3 or 4 weeks, and it will then be ready for use.

CURRANT AND RASPBERRY WINE

To 5 gallons of red-currant juice allow 1 pint of raspberry juice, 10 gallons of water and 10 lb. of either loaf sugar or good preserving sugar.

Extract the juice as directed in the two following recipes.

Add to it the water and sugar, stir until the latter is dissolved, then turn the whole into a cask, and bung closely, but provide the top of the cask with a vent-peg. As soon as fermentation ceases, tighten the vent-peg, and let the cask remain undisturbed in a moderately warm

Cowslip

place for 12 months. At the end of this time rack off into dry bottles, cork them closely, and seal the top with melted wax. The wine should be ready for use in about 3 months.

CURRANT WINE, BLACK

Have ready some ripe black currants. To each pint of juice obtained add 1 pint of cold water, 1 lb. of preserving sugar and a good glass of best brandy.

Take away the stalks, put the currants into an earthenware bowl, bruise well with a wooden spoon, then drain off the juice and put it aside. Add the water to the berries, stir them frequently for 2 or 3 hours, then strain the liquid and mix it with the juice. Add the sugar, and as soon as it is dissolved turn the whole into a cask. When fermentation has ceased rack off the liquid in to a smaller cask, add the brandy, bung closely, and let it remain for at least 12 months in a warm place. At the end of this time drain the wine off carefully into dry bottles, cork them tightly, and store in a dry, moderately warm place.

CURRANT WINE, RED

Procure some ripe red currants. To each gallon of fruit allow 1½ gallons of cold water, 5 lb. either of loaf sugar or good preserving sugar and ½ a pint of good brandy.

Remove the stalks from the currants, put them into an earthenware bowl, bruise them well with a wooden spoon, and drain off the juice. Put the juice aside, add the water to the berries, let it stand for 2 or 3 hours, stirring occasionally meanwhile. At the end of this time strain the liquid from the berries into the juice, add three-quarters of the sugar, stir occasionally until dissolved, then pour the whole into a cask, filling it three parts full. Bung closely, but place a vent-peg near the top of the cask, and let the cask remain for 1 month where a uniform temperature of about 65° Fahr. can be maintained. Dissolve the remainder of the sugar in the smallest possible quantity of warm water, mix it well with the contents of the cask, replace the bung, and allow the cask to remain undisturbed for 6 weeks longer. Now drain off the wine into a clean, dry cask, add the brandy, let the cask stand for about 6 months in a dry, warm place, then bottle and cork tightly. The wine may be used at once, but will be better if kept for 12 months at least.

Note: See also recipes on previous page for Currant and Raspberry, and Black Currant Wine.

DAMSON WINE

To each gallon of damsons add 1 gallon of boiling water. To each gallon of liquor obtained from these add 4 lb. of loaf sugar and ½ a pint of best brandy.

Brandy

Remove the stalks, put the fruit into an earthenware bowl, pour in the boiling water, and cover with a cloth. Stir the liquid three or four times daily for 4 days, then add the sugar and brandy, and when the former is dissolved turn the whole into a clean dry cask. Cover the bung-hole with a cloth, folded into several thicknesses, until fermentation ceases, then bung tightly, and allow the cask to remain undisturbed for 12 months in a moderately warm place. At the end of this time it should be racked off into bottles. The wine may be used at once, but if well corked and stored in a dry place it may be kept for years.

DANDELION WINE

Have ready 4 quarts of dandelion flowers, 4 quarts of boiling water, 3 lb. of loaf sugar, 1 inch of whole ginger, 1 lemon, the thinly-pared rind of 1 orange and 1 tablespoonful of brewers' yeast, or ¼ of an oz. of compressed yeast moistened with water.

Put the petals of the flowers into a bowl, pour over them the boiling water, let the bowl remain covered for 3 days, meanwhile stirring it well and frequently. Strain the liquid into a preserving-pan, add the rinds of the orange and lemon, both of which should be pared off in thin fine strips, the sugar, ginger, and the lemon previously stripped of its white pith and thinly sliced. Boil gently for about ½ an hour, and when cool add the yeast spread on a piece of toast. Allow it to stand for 2 days, then turn it into a cask, keep it well bunged down for 8 or 9 weeks, and bottle the wine for use.

Dandelion

ELDERBERRY WINE

Take 7 lb. of elderberries and 3 gallons of water.

Strip the berries from the stalks, pour the water, quite boiling, over them, let them stand for 24 hours, then bruise well and drain through a hair sieve or jelly-bag. Measure the juice obtained, and to each gallon of liquid allow 3 lb. of good loaf sugar, 1 lb. of raisins, ½ an oz. of ground ginger, 6 cloves, ¼ of a pint of brandy, ½ a teaspoonful of brewers' yeast. Put the juice into a preserving-pan with sugar, raisins, ginger, and cloves, boil gently for about 1 hour, and skim when necessary. Let the liquid stand until milk-warm, then stir in the yeast and turn the whole into a clean, dry cask. Cover the bung-hole with a folded cloth, let the cask remain undisturbed for 14 days, then stir in the brandy and bung tightly. In about 6 months the wine may be drawn off into bottles, tightly corked, and stored for use.

GINGER WINE

Have at hand 3 gallons of cold water, 9 lb. of loaf sugar, ¼ of a lb. of whole ginger bruised, ¼ of a lb. of raisins, the strained juice and finely-pared rinds of 4 lemons, a good tablespoonful of brewers' yeast.

Gooseberries

Stone and halve the raisins, put them into a large preserving-pan of perfectly clean copper, with the water, sugar and ginger bruised; boil for about 1 hour, skimming frequently. Turn the whole into a large earthenware bowl or wooden tub, allow the liquid to stand until milk-warm, then stir in the yeast. On the following day put the preparation into a clean, dry cask, add the lemon-juice, and bung lightly. Stir the wine every day for a fortnight, then tighten the bung. Let the wine remain undisturbed for 3 or 4 months, when it may be bottled for use.

GINGER WINE II

Take 6 gallons of water, 14 lb. of loaf sugar, 6 oz. of whole ginger bruised, 2 lb. of Muscatel raisins, 4 lb. of Valencia raisins, ½ an oz. of isinglass, 6 lemons, 2 tablespoonfuls of yeast and 1 pint of brandy.

Remove the peel of the lemons as thinly as possible, and boil it with the water, sugar and ginger for about ½ an hour. Meanwhile stone and halve the raisins, put them into an earthenware bowl, pour the liquid over them when nearly cold, add the lemon-juice and yeast. Stir it every day for a fortnight, then add the isinglass previously dissolved in a little warm water, and drain into a clean, dry cask. Let the wine remain closely bunged for about 3 months, then bottle for use.

GOOSEBERRY WINE

Procure 20 lb. of firm green gooseberries, 3 gallons of hot water, 15 lb. of loaf sugar and 1½ oz. of cream of tartar.

Top and tail the gooseberries, put them into an earthenware bowl or wooden tub, and pour over them the hot water. Let them soak for 24 hours, then bruise them well with a heavy wooden mallet or potato-masher, and drain the juice through a fine hair sieve or jelly-bag. Replace the skins in the vessel in which they were soaked, cover them with boiling water, stir and bruise well so as to extract the juice completely, then strain through the sieve or bag. Mix this preparation with the juice, add the sugar, and boiling water to increase the liquid to 5 gallons. Replace in the bowl or tub, stir in the cream of tartar, cover with a heavy woollen cloth, and allow the vessel to stand in a moderately warm place for 2 days. Now strain the liquid into a small cask, cover the bung-hole with a folded cloth until fermentation ceases - which may be known by the cessation of the hissing noise - then bung closely, but provide the top of the cask with a vent-peg. Make this wine in the beginning of June, before the berries ripen; let it remain undisturbed until December, then drain it off carefully into a clean cask. In March or April, or when the gooseberry bushes begin to blossom, the wine must be bottled and tightly corked. To ensure its being clear and effervescing, the wine must be bottled at the right time and on a clear day.

GOOSEBERRY WINE II

To each lb. of firm green gooseberries allow 2 pints of cold water. To each gallon of juice obtained from the fruit allow 3 lb. of loaf sugar, ½ a pint of good gin and ¾ oz. of isinglass.

Top and tail the gooseberries, bruise them thoroughly, pour over them the cold water, and let them stand for about 4 days, stirring frequently. Strain through a jelly-bag or fine hair sieve, dissolve the sugar in the liquid, add the gin and isinglass dissolved in a little warm water, and pour the whole into a cask. Bung loosely until fermentation has ceased, then tighten the bung, and let the cask remain undisturbed for at least 6 months. At the end of this time the wine may be bottled, but it will not be ready for use for at least 12 months.

GRAPE WINE

Have ready some sound, not over-ripe grapes and to each lb. allow 1 quart of cold water.

Strip the grapes from the stalks, put them into a wooden tub or earthenware bowl, and bruise them well. Pour over them the water, let them stand for 3 days, stirring frequently, then strain through a jelly-bag or fine hair sieve. To each gallon of liquid obtained from the grapes allow 3 lb. of loaf sugar, ¼ of a pint of French brandy, and about ¼ of an oz. of isinglass. Dissolve the sugar in the liquid, then pour the whole into a cask. Bung lightly for a few days until fermentation subsides, then add the isinglass dissolved in a little warm water, and the brandy, and tighten the bung. Let the cask remain undisturbed for 6 months, then rack the wine off into bottles, cork and seal them securely, and keep for at least a year before using.

Grapes

LEMON FLIP

Take ¼ of a pint of lemon-juice, the rind of 2 lemons, 5 or 6 oz. of castor sugar, 4 eggs, 1 pint of boiling water and about a ¼ of a pint of sherry.

Peel the rind off 2 lemons in the thinnest possible strips. Put them into a jug with the sugar, add the boiling water, and let it stand until cold. Now stir in the well-beaten eggs, the strained lemon-juice and the sherry; strain through a fine strainer, and use as required. It will not keep for any length of time.

LEMON WINE

Take 10 lemons, 4 lb. of loaf sugar, 4 quarts of boiling water and 1 tablespoonful of brewers' yeast.

Remove the rinds of 5 lemons in thin fine strips, and place them in a wooden tub or earthenware bowl. Boil the sugar and water together for about ½ an hour, then pour the syrup over the lemon-peel. When cool add the strained juice of the 10 lemons, stir in the yeast, and let the vessel stand for 48 hours. At the end of this time strain into a cask, which the wine must quite fill, bung loosely until fermentation ceases, then tighten the bung, and allow the cask to remain undisturbed for about 6 months before racking the wine off into bottles.

ORANGE WINE

To the juice of 50 Seville oranges allow 15 lb. of loaf sugar, 4 gallons of water, the whites and shells of 3 eggs, 1 pint of best French brandy and about 3 tablespoonfuls of brewers' yeast.

Dissolve the sugar in the water, add the whites and crushed shells of the eggs, bring to the boil, and simmer gently for about 20 minutes. Let it stand until nearly cold, then strain through a jelly-bag, add the strained orange-juice and yeast and leave the vessel covered for 24 hours. Pour into a cask, bung loosely until fermentation subsides, then tighten the bung, and allow the cask to remain undisturbed for 3 months. At the end of this time rack it off into another cask, add the brandy, let it remain closely bunged for 12 months, then bottle and use as required.

PARSNIP WINE

To 4 lb. of parsnips allow 3 lb. of Demerara sugar, ¼ of an oz. of mild hops, 1 tablespoonful of fresh yeast, 1 slice of toasted bread, and 4 quarts of boiling water.

Boil the parsnips gently in the water for about 15 minutes, add the hops, and cook for about 10 minutes longer. Strain, add the sugar, let the liquid become lukewarm, and put in the toast spread with the yeast. Let it ferment for 36 hours, then turn it into a cask, which it should fill. As soon as fermentation ceases, strain into small bottles, cork securely, and store in a cool, dry place for at least 1 month before using.

RAISIN WINE

To each lb. of raisins allow 1 gallon of cold water, 2 lb. of good preserving sugar and 1 tablespoonful of yeast.

Strip the raisins from the stalks, put them into a large boiler or clean copper with the water, simmer gently for about 1 hour, then rub them through a sieve. Dissolve the sugar in the liquid, and add the raisin-pulp and the yeast, let the vessel stand covered for 3 days, then strain the liquid into a cask. Bung loosely until fermentation ceases,

Parsnip

then tighten the bung, and allow the cask to stand for at least 12 months before racking the wine off into bottles.

RAISIN WINE II

Have at hand 16 lb. of raisins and 2 gallons of water. Strip the raisins from the stalks, put them into an earthenware or wooden vessel, pour over them the water, and let them remain covered for 4 weeks, stirring daily. At the end of this time strain the liquid into a cask which it will quite fill, bung loosely until fermentation subsides, then tighten the bung, and allow the cask to remain undisturbed for 12 months. Now rack it off carefully into another cask, straining the liquid near the bottom of the cask repeatedly until quite clear, let it stand for at least 2 years, and then bottle for use.

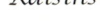

Raisins

RAISIN WINE WITH CIDER

Take 8 gallons of good cider, 15 lb. of Malaga raisins, 1 bottle of good French brandy, 3 oz. of sugar-candy, and the rind and juice of 3 or 4 lemons.

Strip the raisins from the stalks, halve them, put them into a 9-gallon cask, and pour over them the cider. Bung lightly for 5 or 6 days, then tighten the bung and let the cask stand for 6 months. Strain into another cask, passing the liquid near the bottom repeatedly through a jelly-bag or fine muslin until quite clear, add the brandy, the sugar-candy crushed to a powder, and the finely-pared rind and strained juice of the lemons. Keep the wine well bunged for 2 years, then bottle, cork and seal securely, store it in a cool, dry place for one year longer, when it will be ready for use.

RASPBERRY AND CURRANT WINE

Procure 6 quarts of raspberries, 4 quarts of red currants, 10 quarts of water, 10 lb. of good preserving sugar, and 1 pint of French brandy.

Strip the red currants from the stalks, put them into a large earthenware or wooden vessel, and pour over them the water (which must have been previously boiled and allowed to become quite cold). On the following day crush the red currants with a wooden mallet or potato-masher, add the raspberries, and allow the whole to stand until the following day. Strain the liquid through a jelly-bag or fine hair sieve, and drain the fruit thoroughly, but do not squeeze it. Stir in the sugar, and when quite dissolved turn the wine into a clean, dry cask. Bung loosely until fermentation has entirely subsided, then tighten the bung, and allow the cask to remain undisturbed for 3 months. At the end of this time rack the wine off carefully, straining that near the bottom of the cask repeatedly until quite clear. Scald and drain the cask, replace

Rhubarb

the wine, add the brandy, bung lightly, let it remain 2 months longer in the cask, and then bottle.

RASPBERRY VINEGAR

Take 2 quarts of raspberries and 2 quarts of white wine vinegar; to each pint of liquid obtained from these add 1 lb. of loaf or good preserving sugar.

Put the raspberries into a wide-necked glass bottle, or an unglazed jar; pour over them the vinegar; cover, and let the liquid stand for 10 days, stirring it daily. Strain and measure the vinegar: to each pint allow 1 lb. of sugar, and stir occasionally till the sugar is dissolved. Pour the whole into a jar, place the jar in a saucepan of boiling water, and simmer gently for 1¼ hours, skimming when necessary. When cold, bottle for use.

RASPBERRY WINE

To 10 quarts of ripe raspberries allow 10 quarts of boiling water, 6 lb. of good preserving sugar, 2 tablespoonfuls of brewers' yeast, 1 pint of French brandy and ¼ of an oz. of isinglass.

Prepare the fruit in the usual way, put it into an earthenware or wooden vessel, pour over it the boiling water, and let it remain covered until the following day. Pass both liquid and fruit through a fine hair sieve, let it stand for 24 hours, then strain it carefully, without disturbing the sediment, into another vessel. Add the sugar, stir in the yeast, and as soon as the sugar is dissolved turn the whole into a clean, dry cask. Cover the bung-hole with a folded cloth until fermentation subsides, then bung it closely. Let it stand for 1 month, rack it off into a clean cask, add the brandy, and isinglass dissolved in a little warm water, bung tightly, and allow it to remain undisturbed for 12 months. At the end of this time rack it off into bottles, cork securely, store for 12 months longer, and the wine will be ready for use.

RASPBERRY WINE II

Procure 6 quarts of ripe raspberries and 6 quarts of water.

Put the raspberries into an earthenware or wooden vessel, bruise them well with a heavy wooden spoon, and pour over them the cold water. Let them stand until the following day, stirring them frequently, then strain the liquid through a jelly-bag or fine hair sieve, and drain the fruit thoroughly, but avoid squeezing it. Measure the liquid; to each quart add 1 lb. of loaf sugar; stir occasionally until dissolved, then turn the whole into a cask. Bung loosely for several days, until fermentation ceases, then tighten the bung, let it remain thus for 3 months, and bottle for use.

RHUBARB WINE

Have ready 25 lb. of rhubarb and 5 gallons of cold water.

Wipe the rhubarb with a damp cloth, and cut it into short lengths, leaving on the peel. Put it into an earthenware or wooden vessel, crush it thoroughly with a wooden mallet or heavy potato-masher, and pour over it the water. Let it remain covered for 10 days, stirring it daily; then strain and measure the liquor into another vessel. To each gallon of liquid add 3 lb. of either loaf or good preserving sugar, and the juice and very thinly-pared rind of 1 lemon, and stir occasionally until the sugar is dissolved. Now put it into a cask, and add to the whole 1 oz. of isinglass previously dissolved in a little warm water; cover the bung-hole with a folded cloth for 10 days, then bung securely, and allow it to remain undisturbed for 12 months. At the end of this time rack off into bottles, and use.

WELSH NECTAR

Take ½ a lb. of raisins, 1 lb. of loaf sugar, 2 small lemons, and 4 quarts of boiling water.

Remove the rinds of the lemons as thinly as possible, and pour over them the boiling water. When cool, add the strained juice of the lemons, the raisins stoned and finely-chopped, and the sugar. Cover; let the preparation remain for 5 days, stirring three or four times daily, then strain into bottles. This beverage will keep good only a short time.

Luncheon Still Life by John F. Francis (circa 1860)

CHAPTER XIV

LIQUEURS

ANISE LIQUEUR

Have ready 1 quart of good brandy, 1 oz. of anise-seed, 1 lb. of loaf sugar and 1 pint of water.

Put the anise-seed into the brandy, and let it stand, closely corked, for a fortnight, shaking it occasionally; boil the sugar and water to a syrup, and strain the brandy into it. When cool, pour into dry, clean bottles, cork securely, and store for use.

ARRACK LIQUEUR

To 1 quart of arrack allow 1 quart of water, 1 lb. of sugar-candy, and the rind of ½ a lemon.

Remove the outer part of the lemon-rind as thinly as possible, add it and the sugar-candy to the water, and boil gently until a moderately thick syrup is formed. When cold, strain and add it to the arrack, bottle, cork securely, and store for use.

ARRACK

This spirit is produced by fermenting the juice of the cocoa and other palms; it is extensively used in the East, but is little known in England.

BLACK-CURRANT LIQUEUR

Procure 1 lb. of black currants, ¾ of a lb. of brown sugar-candy, and 1½ pints of good gin.

Strip the fruit from the stalks, put it into a wide-necked bottle, add the sugar-candy crushed to a fine powder, and pour in the gin. Let it stand for 2 months, then strain until it is quite clear, rack off in to bottles, seal and store in a cool, dry place until required.

CARAWAY LIQUEUR

Take 1 oz. of caraway seeds, ½ a lb. of loaf sugar, 1 quart of brandy and ½ a pint of water.

Boil the sugar and water to thin syrup, pour it, quite boiling, over the caraway seeds, let it cool slightly, and add the brandy. When quite cold pour the whole into a bottle, cork securely, allow it to stand for 10 days, then strain into small bottles, cork them tightly, and store in a cool, dry place until required.

CHERRY BRANDY

To each lb. of sound Morello cherries allow 3 oz. of brown sugar-candy, 12 apricot, peach, or plum kernels, ¼ of an oz. of shredded bitter almond, ¼ of an inch of cinnamon, and good French brandy to cover.

Cut off the stalks, leaving them about ½ an inch in length, wipe the cherries with a soft cloth, and prick them well with a coarse darning needle; half fill some wide-necked bottles with the prepared fruit; to each one add sugar-candy, etc., in the above-stated proportions, and fill the bottles with brandy. Cork closely, cover the top with melted wax or bladder, and keep for at least 3 months before using. Shake the bottle well at intervals.

CHERRY LIQUEUR

Remove the stalks and stones from 1 lb. of Morello cherries and 1 lb. of black cherries, crush the stones and cherries, put them into a bottle with ½ a lb. of loaf or good preserving sugar, ¼ of an oz. of stick cinnamon, 12 cloves, and pour over them brandy. Cork closely, let it stand for 14 days, then strain into small bottles, cork securely, and store in a cool, dry place.

CITRON LIQUEUR

Remove the rinds of 4 lemons as thinly as possible, pour over them 1 pint of spirits of wine or gin, cover and put aside for 10 days. On the tenth day make 1 pint of syrup, add the strained juice of 4 lemons and, when quite cold, strain and mix in the spirits of wine or gin. Bottle, cork securely, and store for use.

CLOVE LIQUEUR

Take ¼ of a lb. of cloves, ¼ of a lb. of coriander seed, ½ a lb. of loaf sugar, 2 dozen large black cherries and 1 quart of gin or brandy.

Remove the stalks and stones from the cherries, bruise the stones, also the cloves and coriander seed. Put the whole into a wide-necked bottle, add the sugar, pour in the brandy and cover closely for 1 month. When ready, strain the liquid into small bottles, cover closely, and store for use.

CURAÇOA

Procure 1 quart of brandy or rectified spirits of wine, 1 lb. of loaf sugar, ½ a pint of cold water, ½ a pint of boiling water, and 2 oz. of very thinly-pared orange-rind.

Put the orange-rinds into a jar, pour over them the boiling water; when cool, add the brandy. Cover closely, let the liquid stand for 10 days in a moderately warm place, and stir it two or three times daily. On the tenth day boil the sugar and cold water together until reduced to a thick syrup, let this become quite cold, then add to it the liquid from the jar previously strained through flannel or fine muslin until clear. Pour into small bottles, cork tightly, and store.

DAMSON GIN (*See* Sloe Gin)

FOUR FRUIT LIQUEUR

Have at hand ¾ of a lb. of strawberries, ¾ of a lb. of Kentish cherries, ½ a lb. of raspberries and ½ a lb. of black currants.

Strip the fruit from the stalks, put it into a jar, stand the latter in a saucepan of boiling water, and cook gently for about 1 hour. Strain the juice through a jelly-bag, being careful not to press the pulp, and to each pint of strained juice add ½ a pint of French brandy, 3 oz. of loaf sugar, and half the cherry kernels. Cover closely, let the liqueur stand for 3 days, then strain it into small bottles, and cork them securely.

GINGER BRANDY

Procure 2 oz. of Jamaica ginger, 1 quart of brandy, ½ a pint of water, 1 lb. of sugar and 2 oz. of juniper berries (mixed black and white).

Crush finely the ginger and juniper berries, put them into a wide-necked bottle, and pour in the brandy. Cork securely, let the bottle stand in a warm place for 3 days, shaking it three or four times daily. On the third day boil the sugar and water to a thick syrup, and when cool add to it the brandy, which must previously be strained through fine muslin or filtering paper until quite clear. When quite cold pour into clean, dry bottles, cork securely, and store in a cool place until required for use.

HAWTHORN LIQUEUR

Have ready some white hawthorn blossoms and sufficient good brandy to cover.

Gather the blossoms on a dry day, put them into wide-necked bottles, shaking, but not pressing, them down. Fill the bottles with brandy, cork them securely, let them remain thus for 4 months, then strain the liqueur into small bottles, and cork tightly. This liqueur is used chiefly for flavouring creams, custards, etc.

LEMON GIN (*See* Citron Liqueur)

Hawthorn

Almonds

NOYEAU (IMITATION)

Take 3 oz. of bitter almonds, 2 oz. of sweet almonds, 1 lb. of loaf sugar, 1 quart of brandy or gin and 2 tablespoonfuls of honey.

Blanch the almonds, pound them well in a mortar, or chop them very finely, put them into a clean wide-necked bottle or jar, pour into them the spirit, and cover closely. Keep the jar in a moderately cool place for 3 days, shaking frequently, then add the honey and sugar, and stir occasionally until they are dissolved. Strain through very fine muslin into small bottles, and cork them securely. Store in a cool, dry place. Apricot, nectarine, or peach kernels can be used instead of the almonds.

Note: Noyeau (or Noyau) is a French liqueur made from brandy flavoured with almonds and apricot kernels.

NOYEAU (IMITATION) II

Have at hand 3 pints of French brandy, ½ a pint of boiling milk, 1½ lb. of loaf sugar, 4 oz. of bitter almonds, $\frac{1}{8}$ of an oz. of stick cinnamon and 1 lemon.

Remove the rind of the lemon as thinly as possible, put it into a wide-necked bottle, add the sugar, cinnamon, almonds blanched, and the juice of ½ the lemon. Shake occasionally until the sugar is dissolved, then add the milk, quite boiling, and when cold add the brandy and cover closely. Shake the bottle three or four times a day for 3 weeks, then strain into small bottles, cork securely, and store for use.

ORANGE BRANDY

To 2 quarts of French brandy allow ¾ of a pint of orange juice, the rind of 6 oranges and 1¼ lb. of loaf sugar.

Remove the rinds of 6 oranges as thinly as possible, mix the strained orange-juice and brandy together, add the prepared rinds and sugar, and turn the whole into a wide-necked bottle. Cork closely, shake it two or three times daily for about 30 days, then strain into small bottles, and store in a cool place.

ORANGE LIQUEUR

Take the peel of 3 Seville oranges, 1½ pints of gin or rectified spirits of wine, 1 lb. of loaf sugar, ¼ of a pint of water and a pinch of saffron.

Remove the rinds of the oranges in fine strips, and put them into a wide-necked bottle or jar, with the saffron and gin. Boil the sugar and water to a thick syrup; when cool add it to the contents of the bottle. Cover closely and let it remain in a moderately warm place for a month. Then strain into small bottles, cork securely, and store in a cool cellar.

RASPBERRY BRANDY

To 1 pint of ripe raspberries allow 1 quart of French brandy, ¼ of a lb. of loaf sugar and about 2 tablespoonfuls of cold water.

Put the raspberries into a wide-necked bottle, pour the brandy over them, cork the bottle tightly, and let it stand in a moderately warm place for 14 days. Have ready a thick syrup, made by boiling together the sugar and water until the right consistency is obtained. Strain the liquor from the bottle repeatedly until quite clear, then mix it with the syrup, and pour the whole into small bottles. Cork them securely, and store for use.

RASPBERRY GIN

To 1 quart of ripe raspberries add 1 quart of good gin and 1 lb. of sugar-candy.

Break the sugar-candy in small pieces, put it into a jar with the raspberries and gin, cover closely, and let it remain thus for 12 months, shaking it daily for three or four weeks. At the end of the time strain or filter until clear, and bottle for use.

RATAFIA

Have ready 4 oz. of cherry kernels, preferably those taken from Morello cherries, 1 oz. of apricot or peach kernels, 1 bottle of good brandy, ½ a lb. of sugar-candy, and ¼ of a pint of cold water.

Pound the kernels until smooth, moistening them from time to time with a few drops of brandy. Put them with the remainder of the brandy into a wide-necked bottle, cover closely and shake two or three times daily for 6 weeks. Strain the liqueur first through fine muslin and afterwards through filtering-paper, add to it the sugar-candy finely powdered and dissolved in cold water, bottle, cork tightly, and store for use.

SHRUB

To ½ a gallon of rum allow ¾ of a pint of orange-juice, ½ a pint of lemon-juice, the peel of 2 lemons, 2 lb. of loaf sugar and 2 ½ pints of water.

Slice the lemon-peel very thinly, and put it, with the fruit juice and spirit, in a large covered jar. Let it stand for 2 days, then pour over it the water in which the sugar has been dissolved, take out the lemon-peel, and leave it for 12 days before using.

SLOE GIN

Half fill clean, dry wine bottles with sloes previously pricked with a darning needle. Add to each 1oz. of crushed barley-sugar, a little noyeau, or 2 or 3 drops of essence of almonds.

Sloes

Fill the bottles with good unsweetened gin, cork them securely, and allow them to remain in a moderately warm place for 3 months. At the end of this time strain the liqueur through fine muslin or filtering-paper until quite clear, then bottle it, cork securely, and store for use.

STRAWBERRY LIQUEUR

Half fill wide-necked glass bottles with ripe strawberries previously pricked with a darning-needle, put an equal portion of finely-crushed sugar-candy into each, and fill them with good brandy. Cork tightly, allow them to stand in a warm place for 6 weeks, then strain the liquid into small bottles, cork securely, and store for use.

VANILLA LIQUEUR

Take 2 Vanilla pods, 3 pints of brandy or gin, 1 lb. of loaf sugar and 1 pint of water.

Break the pods into short lengths, put them into the spirit, cork closely, and let it infuse for 14 days. On the last day boil the sugar and water to a thick syrup, strain the spirit into it, and when quite cold bottle for use.

Still Life by Albert Anker (1831-1910)

*Stillleben mit Pflaumen [Still Life with Plums]
by August Herrmann-Allgäu (1911)*

Plate from *Mrs Beeton's Book of Household Management*

DESSERT.

Plate from *Mrs Beeton's Book of Household Management*

VINTAGE WORDS OF WISDOM

Rosemary for Remembering

The Vintage Words of Wisdom titles are not simply facsimiles of old books. They have been carefully selected and professionally produced as high quality ebooks and print books. Our aim is to make the best vintage books on popular topics of interest more widely available again. The books range from practical titles that include wisdom from times past to unashamedly nostalgic works that will appeal to those who may remember these or similar titles from their childhood. Often amusing and quaint, these vintage volumes also contain wise words and advice that may have been forgotten in the intervening years. So often it is worth revisiting the past to remind ourselves that the best ideas stand the test of time. Above all, the Vintage Words of Wisdom titles are highly entertaining and provide a fascinating snapshot of life in days gone by. We have chosen books with wonderful illustrations, exciting stories of daring and adventure, practical advice and charming nostalgic descriptions of a simpler life.

Titles include:
- *Poultry-keeping*
- *Room and Window Gardening*
- *Ferns and Fern Culture*
- *Woodwork Tools and How to Use Them* (ebook and print editions)
- *Home Carpentry: A Practical Guide for the Amateur*
- *The Boys' Book of Aeroplanes*
- *The Railway Age*
- *Sky Roads of the World*
- *Lillie London's Needlework Book*
- *The Cottage Farm Month by Month*
- *Mrs Beeton's Jam-making and Preserves* (ebook and print editions)

Heath Robinson titles:
- *How to Live in a Flat*
- *How to be a Motorist*
- *How to Make a Garden Grow*
- *How to be a Perfect Husband*
- *Humours of Golf*

For further details and the most up-to-date information on our titles please visit our website www.wordstothewise.co.uk